AF879744

YOUR PRACTICAL GUIDE FOR MARRIAGE BASED IMMIGRATION

IT'S NOT JUST FORMS

IMMIGRATION LAWYER SERIES: BOOK 2

FIRST EDITION

TONI GILLIARD, ESQ

Your Practical Guide for Marriage Based Immigration
Immigration Lawyer Series: Book 2
First Edition
© 2016 by Toni Gilliard, Esq.

All rights reserved. No part of this book may be used or reproduced by any means, graphic, electronic, or mechanical, including photocopying, recording, taping or by any information storage retrieval system without the written permission of the author except in the case of brief quotations embodied in critical articles and reviews.

ISBN 978-0-692-65980-9

Printed in the United States of America.

Easy Immigration Publications
www.EasyImmigrationPublications.com

Designed by King's Daughter Publishing
www.KingsDaughterPublishing.com

DEDICATION

This book is dedicated to my children – Ryan Pilar Husser and Jonathan L. Husser, III. You have reminded me every day to always find a way and to create the life I envisioned for myself without asking for permission.

I love you with every fiber of my soul.

PREFACE

Welcome to marriage-based immigration. Whether you are a new lawyer or a practicing attorney interested in marriage based immigration you will find the information useful. As a practicing attorney, you may represent a client who is divorced and remarrying a foreign national or have a client who is a foreign national who would like to divorce their spouse who is a United States Citizen. And on the other hand, you may have a United Staes Citizen client seeking to divorce a foreign national based on fraud or misrepresentation in an attempt to get their green card.

Like many lawyers, new and seasoned, the job opportunities for lawyers are declining as the dynamics are changing in the legal arena. Many lawyers are finding themselves in private practice. Some are in private practice by choice and others by circumstances. Offering immigration services is an excellent way to add to your practice area(s). While immigration law is very diverse and varies, it will allow you to offer an added value to your practice. Immigration law merges well with other practice areas and ranges from business immigration, deportation defense, to family based. Within those broad immigration areas are other niche areas as well. Within business immigration there is I-9 compliance and business visas for corporations large and small. Within family immigration, there is adoption and marriage based. This guide covers a narrow market of marriage-based immigration visas.

This guide is part of a series of immigration manuals and guides for lawyers. Your Practical Guide for Marriage Based Immigration: It's Not Just Forms, is Book 2 in the Immigration Lawyer Series.

How to Use This Book

Have you been representing people for years and immigration law questions arise, but you have never practiced immigration law? Do you want to open an immigration practice or add immigration to your list of services but don't know where to start? This guide offers an overview of Marriage-based Immigration Law in the United States. This guide focuses on Marriage-based Immigration law basics (state-side filings) and essential analytical skills needed to zealously advocate for your client before USCIS local offices.

Contents

1

Getting Clients

If you are a practicing attorney you already have access to potential clientele. You simply have to let your current client base know that you are offering marriage-based immigration services. You can, of course, do this by word of mouth, which I find to be the best form, of advertisement. You can also do a mass mailing in form of a letter or postcards letting them know about the added service. There are other ways such as updating your website, SEO, e-newsletters and other print advertisements as well.

As a newbie, whether seasoned in other areas of law or new to law practice in general, you must get the word out regarding the services you provide. Try advertising in foreign periodicals, television, or radio. Giving of yourself pays off in the end. Writing a free column on the topic or offering to answer questions live on air will bring in business. You will be looked at as an expert in the community. However, be careful not to advertise as an expert or specialist if you are not. Check with your local bar rules regarding advertisement Rules of Professional Conduct. Not every state has an immigration specialization. Speaking to ethnic groups and organizations for free is an excellent way to get new clients. Remember you have to give in order to receive. If you are interested in immigration, you likely have a giving spirit.

The immigrant population is very diverse. You do not need to speak a foreign language to practice immigration law. There are many successful immigration attorneys throughout the United States who do not speak another language. If there is a particular ethnic group you desire to represent, you can hire someone to translate and interpret for you. If your budget does not permit you to hire staff, you can always utilize contract services of local interpreters on an as needed basis, translators over the phone or require that the client bring their own interpreter. Knowing your target market will help hone your focus. If your market speaks a certain language, you know that you must either speak the language or hire staff who do.

Whether you are just opening your doors or expanding your operation, it is imperative that you educate yourself about your field of choice. Join your local immigration bar or American Immigration Lawyers Association (AILA). Attend Continuing Legal Education events where you will be able to network with practicing attorneys of small, midsize and large practices.

Attend local immigration bar meetings and national conferences at least twice a year. The local meetings will keep you informed about jurisdictional policies and procedures and connected you with other immigration attorneys. Having a relationship with your local chapter members allows you access to free mentorships. Mentors will provide you with practical advice and will likely help you generate income. At times, your colleagues will call upon you to cover a hearing at immigration court or at the immigration office. When you are facing scheduling conflicts, you can call upon someone to cover a hearing for you. Colleagues are also excellent referral sources. Not all practitioners take every case that walks through the door. There may be attorneys who practice exclusively within their niche area of law and will refer other matters to you.

Speaking engagements will help get new clients. Unless you plan on opening an office and hiring other attorneys to do the work and book the clients, you will have to talk to clients. You will have to get the word out that you are practicing immigration. Speaking for free at churches, religious institutions and community events will be key. I call this "grassroots" marketing. Direct mail marketing may not work within the immigration field. People need to see you and, in some cases, feel you. Immigration law is based on trust first! So get out there! What are you waiting for?

2

Screening Clients

Once you have gotten your first immigration client it is important to screen them properly. You do not want to take on a case that you cannot file because (a) your client is not eligible for the relief you promised or (b) filing the case will land the client in Removal (deportation) proceedings. That is a fast track way of getting a grievance complaint and possible civil law suit.

A sample Intake sheet is included in the Appendix.

Basic information you need to obtain:

Question 1. Name, address, phone number, email: This information is important for record keeping and communication as well as your client mailing list for future marketing.

Question 2. A#: The "A number" is a number assigned by immigration services. If your client has an "A number" it is a Red flag. This means they have had some form of contact with immigration services. They may have filed a petition, been placed in proceedings for removal, or have a petition pending.

Ask your potential client if he/she has had any contact with immigration ever "in life" or has he/she filed or had someone file "anything" with immigration. This is very important! You do not want to file a new case for your client to have it later denied because of a deportation history. The petition may be able to be filed, but there may be necessary prerequisites like reopening the deportation case first or motions to reopen and reconsider. If there is a prior revocation or denial of a petition, you may be able to file an appeal or motion to reopen and reconsider with USCIS.[1]

If your client has an "A number" I strongly suggest you do a FOIA first before accepting the case.[2] Many times, a client may have had a fraudulent case filed by a nonlawyer/notario, filed themselves or by a family member.[3] Many times they had fraudulent petitions filed with a promise to get a work permit. The client may have filed for Asylum or other relief they didn't qualify for. You do not want to awake that demon! Your client may have a final order of deportation in absentia[4] and may be picked up by ICE.[5]

Question 3. How did the foreign national enter the USA?:

(A) If they entered legally with a work visa, student visa, tourist

---

1 USCIS: United States Citizenship and Immigration Services.

2 FOIA: Freedom of Information Act/Privacy Act Request. Form G-639.

3 Notario: Notarios are not lawyers. Notario is Spanish for Notary Public "notario publico." Notarios are not valid accredited representatives approved by the U.S. government. The term "notario publico" may be seen advertised in the Hispanic community. That title is not recognized in the United States as it is in some Latin American countries.

4 In absentia: Ordered removed/deported while not present at immigration court.

5 ICE: Immigration and Customs Enforcement.

visa, or any other visa other than a crewman (worked on a ship) you are safe to proceed.

(B) If they enter as a crewman they will need to qualify for 245(i) Provision of the Life Act.[6]

(C) When did they enter? You will need to check the entry stamp in their passport. A few years ago, an I-94 card was issued by customs and border patrol. The I-94 card contained the stamp of date and location of admission into the United States and the date the authorized stay expired. Today I-94 cards are not provided and one must go online to retrieve the I-94 data.[7] In some cases the I-94 cannot be retrieved. Your best proof of lawful entry into the USA is the passport which contains the visa. Look for the entry stamp. See Appendix for sample I-94 card.[8]

(D) Verify if their status states "No COS/EOS" as this means they are not permitted to Change their status or Extend their status in the USA. Red flag!

(E) Verify when they entered the USA. If they entered the USA less than 90 days ago and married and are attempting to file a marriage based petition, USCIS will suspect marriage fraud. Red flag! There is a presumption of "dual intent" and the case may be denied

---

6 INA section 245(i).Section 245(i) allows certain persons, who have an immigrant visa immediately available but entered without inspection or otherwise violated their status and thus are ineligible to apply for adjustment of status in the United States, to apply if they pay a $1,000 penalty. The LIFE Act temporarily extends the ability to preserve eligibility for this provision of law until April 30, 2001. Use of Section 245(i) adjustment of status previously was limited to eligible individuals who were the beneficiary of a visa petition or labor certification application filed on or before January 14, 1998.

7 www.cbp.gov/I94

8 Form I-102 Application for Replacement/Initial Nonimmigrant Arrival-Departure Document can also be filed.

and your client may be placed in Removal proceedings. Dual intent simply means you had other intentions when entering the United States other than visiting, studying, or working. Your intent was to marry and remain in the USA.[9]

Question 4. Has the foreign national or the USC spouse ever been married?: If so you will need EVERY divorce decree for every terminated marriage. If widowed, you will need the death certificate. Many clients married abroad don't consider themselves married since they were not married in the USA. This is incorrect.

(A) If clients have a foreign divorce decree, you must verify that the divorce is valid. If the divorce is not valid under that country's laws the subsequent USA marriage will not be recognized for immigration purposes.

(B) Proxy marriages and proxy divorces are not recognized under USA immigration laws. In some countries, a family member can "stand" on your behalf and marry or divorce. Under USA immigration laws, YOU need to be physically present for your own marriage or divorce. As an immigration lawyer you may need to contact a local attorney in that country with whom to consult. Charge the client for this service, as you may be required to pay for local counsel advice or services.[10]

---

9 Dual Intent: Arises when non-immigrant visa holders who may want to apply for a Change of Status or Adjustment of Status but doing so, it brings into question whether or not the applicant had a "preconceived intent" at the time that they were granted their non-immigrant visa a short time after entry (30/60/90 day rule). According to the Department of State's Foreign Affairs Manual (9 FAM 40.63, N 4.7), the 30/60-day rule is meant to be used for guidance only, since it is not governed by the statutes or regulations.

10 Proxy marriages: A proxy marriage is a marriage where someone stands in for the other party. That is, either the bride or the groom is not physically present for the wedding. During the solemnization of the marriage, based upon a power of attorney, an

(C) Someone may be married under the foreign country's law although no ceremony took place. In some countries if one lives with, has children and are held out to the public as married, USA immigration laws will require an actual divorce. As a family law attorney you may have to handle an international divorce first before your clients can marry in the USA and subsequently file the Petition for Lawful Permanent Residency.

(D) Same Sex Marriages are now recognized under US Immigration law.[11]

Question 5. Is the Petitioning spouse a US Citizen?:

Note: Lawful Permanent Residents may petition for their Foreign National spouse as well.[12]

Although this may seem like a simple question you will be amazed at how many people believe they are an American citizen and are not. You may also find the opposite, where persons do not believe they are US citizens and they are, under immigration laws.

(A) One way to verify if someone is a US citizen is by birth certificate. Another way to verify US citizenship is by US passport. If someone has Naturalized, they are a US citizen. If someone's par-

---

agent acts on behalf of one of the parties. Proxy marriages are not recognized under immigration law.

11 Same Sex Marriage:In June 2013, the United States Supreme Court ruled that Section III of the Defense of Marriage Act (DOMA) was unconstitutional. This effectively required federal agencies to recognize same-sex marriages. Shortly after the ruling, President Obama directed all federal departments and agencies, including U.S. Citizenship and Immigration Services (USCIS), to implement the ruling swiftly and smoothly.

12 Lawful permanent residents of the USA may Petition for Foreign national spouse. Certain rules apply as well as visa availability. Unlike the petitioning process with US citizen's petitioning for their spouse where the visa is automatically available and not subject to visa availability for immediate relatives.

ent naturalized when they were a lawful permanent resident under the age of 21, they technically are a derivative US citizen.

(B) If the Petitioning spouse was born in Puerto Rico or any United States territory, they may petition for their alien relative.

Spouses of United States citizens are Immediate Relatives therefore there is NO WAITING PERIOD.[13]

I. Criminal History: If your Foreign national has been arrested for any reason, STOP and contact a Criminal Immigration lawyer – Crimigration. You will need the Disposition for all arrests for the Criminal immigration attorney to review before you can file. Failure to do so may land your client in Removal Proceedings (also known as Deportation). Red flag!

II. Is the marriage BONA FIDE "Real"?

If at any point your potential clients says they are simply marrying for the green card you should STOP!!!!! This is marriage Fraud. Even if no gift of money is exchanged, it is marriage fraud.[14] A friend "helping" a friend obtain a green card to stay in the United States is still a violation of immigration laws. This is considered

---

13 Immediate relatives are also widow or widower of a US citizen, parents of a US citizen if the citizen is at least 21 years of age, children of a US citizen under 21 years old (stepchildren and adopted children who were adopted before they were 16 years old).

14 Marriage Fraud: In 1986 United States Congress passed the Immigration Marriage Fraud Amendment. If it is found that an American citizen or lawful permanent resident conspired with a foreign national to circumvent immigration laws by means of Fraudulent marriage they may face Federal sanction such as imprisonment up to five years and fines up to $250,000 or both. The foreign national can be deported as well as the permanent resident who is attempting to file for the foreign national. If found to have committed marriage fraud the foreign national may be barred from filing for any immigration relief in the future. This is commonly referred to as the 204(C) bar.

Marriage Fraud. Bona fide means that the marriage is based on love and a desire to create a life together with your spouse. It must be a legal marriage and valid and recognized by the laws of the state or country in which you married. Parties are not required to marry in the state in which they live or file their case. Your marriage simply has to be recognized under US immigration law. You can marry in another state or in another country and live in another state in which you file. You simply need to present tangible proof such as Marriage certificate to prove that you are married and that your marriage is recognized under Federal Immigration laws.

DUAL REPRESENTATION

Make sure that you follow your local bar rules related to Dual Representation. You are representing both the US citizen and the foreign national in marriage based cases. Be sure to consult with your local bar rules regarding notice requirements and conflict of interest related issues in the event a conflict arises.

You may have a US citizen client who later decides to withdraw the petition filed, leaving your foreign national client out of status and subject to removal from the United States.

3

Gathering the Necessary Documents

The following documents set the process in motion to prove your client is eligible for lawful permanent resident status.

Petitioner — US citizen:

☐ Copy of US Birth Certificate for Petitioner and/or Naturalization certificate
☐ Copy of biographical page of US Passport for Petitioner
☐ Copy of Marriage Certificate.
☐ Copy of Divorce Decree(s) if any
☐ 2- color photos – Passport style

Beneficiary — Foreign National:

☐ Copy of birth certificate
☐ Translation for Birth Certificate if necessary

☐ Copy of biographical page of US Passport for Petitioner
☐ Copy of Divorce Decree(s)
☐ Copy of I-94 or Visa Biographic page with lawful entry stamp *(Color copy not required but suggested)*
☐ Medicals from Designated Civil Surgeon
☐ 4-6 - color photos – Passport style (See USCIS website for photograph requirement). See Appendix
☐ *Any document not in English must be translated and include a Certificate of Translation.
☐ Filing Fees: $420 and $1,070 checks payable to Department of Homeland Security. Note: This is subject to change.[1]
☐ Joint documents proving you have a Bona Fide Marriage

It is important to prove to USCIS that the marriage is real!

1 www.uscis.gov

4

FILING YOUR CASE

The following documents set the process in motion to prove your client is eligible for lawful permanent resident status.

Petitioner — US citizen:

☐ Copy of US Birth Certificate for Petitioner and/or Naturalization certificate
☐ Copy of biographical page of US Passport for Petitioner
☐ Copy of Marriage Certificate.
☐ Copy of Divorce Decree(s) if any
☐ Two (2) color photos – Passport style

Beneficiary — Foreign National:

☐ Copy of birth certificate
☐ Translation for Birth Certificate if necessary
☐ Copy of biographical page of US Passport for Petitioner
☐ Copy of Divorce Decree(s)

☐ Copy of I-94 or Visa Biographic page with lawful entry stamp *(Color copy not required but suggested)*
☐ Medicals from Designated Civil Surgeon
☐ 4-6 - color photos – Passport style (See USCIS website for photograph requirement). See Appendix
☐ Any document not in English must be translated and include a Certificate of Translation.
☐ Filing Fees: $420 and $1,070 checks payable to Department of Homeland Security. Note: This is subject to change.
☐ Proving you have a Bona Fide Marriage

It is important to prove to USCIS that the marriage is real! Enclose joint documents with your filing.

Filing Your Case:
☐Copy of any joint documents reflecting married e.g. deeds, mortgage, utility bills, rental contract, life insurance, auto insurance, health insurance, bank statements;
☐Copy of child of marriage birth certificate;
☐Pictures (copies are fine) of family together, e.g. wedding, holiday, birthdays, etc.

Proof of income from Petitioner is required:
☐Letter of Employment – Sponsor/USC SPOUSE
☐(3 years tax Transcript) IRS Form 1040 with matching W-2 for Sponsor and recent pay stub (last 4);
☐Foreign national and US citizen Joint tax returns if not recent ly married; and
☐If married but filed taxes separate, include both party's recent tax returns for the most recent year.

Forms needed:
☐G-1145: This will allow USCIS to notify you via text and email of their receipt of your petition.

☐ G-28: Notice of Appearance as Attorney of Record: You can not communicate with USCIS without this form being signed by the Attorney of Record and the clients individually. USCIS will not mail you the receipt notices or any notices in reference to your clients' case if this form is not filed with original signatures.
☐ I-130: Petition for Alien Relative
☐ I-485: Application to Adjust Status to Lawful Permanent Resident Status
☐ I-765: Application for Employment Authorization
☐ I-131: Advance Parole Travel Permit
☐ G-325A: Biographic for US citizen (in quadruplicate)
☐ G-325A: Biographic for Foreign National (in quadruplicate)
☐ I-864: Affidavit of Support (signed by Petitioner in BLACK INK ONLY)
☐ I864EZ: Affidavit of Support (If Petitioner meets income requirement with W-2 alone). If using I-864EZ you do not need the I-864
☐ Sealed Envelope of Medicals from Civil Surgeon

Joint Sponsors:
☐ I-864: Affidavit of Support -Completed by Joint Sponsor, if Petitioning US citizen spouse does not meet income requirement
☐ I-864A: Contract between Household member and Sponsor
☐ Proof of Joint Sponsors' status (Copy of Birth Certificate/Naturalization Certificate, Green Card, Driver's license, social security card)
☐ Letter of Employment
☐ (3 years tax Transcript) IRS Form 1040 with matching W-2 for Sponsor and recent pay stub (last four)

- Provide copies of supporting documents listed above.
- Passport style photos. (You must write with a pencil or pen the last name, first name on the back of each photo. DO NOT

STAPLE the photos to the forms. Place in a clear small envelope and attach to cover letter.)
- Separate checks should be made payable to Department of Homeland Security for $420 and $1,070

Caveat: If newly married many documents may not have both party's name. Include what you can as you can supplement at the interview.

Caveat: If your clients are newly married, include three letters/affidavits from family members and/or family that state they know your clients as a married couple. This letter should be written by each party and notarized. The letter must contain the name, address and phone number of the person writing the affidavit.

USCIS officials may contact the individuals if investigating whether your clients' marriage is "real" so make sure the clients are aware and advice those submitting affidavits.

Caveat: The I-765 Should ALWAYS be filed. This will allow your client to obtain a valid Work Authorization Card and a Social Security Card if they do not already have one. Most states require the work authorization and social security card to apply for a Driver's license. The Work Authorization card is also re-quired for employment in the United States. Most states have implemented E-verify.[1]

Caveat: The I-131 Advance Parole should only be filed with the case where the client's authorized stay in the United States has not expired. While the I-130 and I-485 concurrent filing may be filed along with the request for work authorization, I never recommend Travel outside the United States while ones case is pending where their authorized stay has expired. Although USCIS may grant your client's request for Advance Parole, if your client departs the United

1 E-verify: E-Verify is an Internet-based system that allows businesses to determine the eligibility of their employees to work in the United States. U.S. law requires companies to employ individuals who may legally work in the United States – either U.S. citizens, or foreign citizens who have the necessary work authorization.

States, the will not be permitted toreenter. They will be subject to the bars for readmission up-to 10 years.

Example 1: Aileen entered the USA on a B-1 Visa to visit Charleston, SC. She has a visa valid for 10 years, however her I-94/Entry stamp indicates she can only come to the USA for 6 months for this recent trip. While on vacation she meets Uriel a United States Citizen. It was love at first site. He proposes to Aileen and they marry one month before her authorized stay expires. If you are filing this case before her stay expires (NOT HER VISA EXPIRATION), you should file for Advance Parole Form I-131. If Aileen needs to leave the USA after filing her case, she can return to the USA on her Advance Parole.[2]

Example 2: Aileen entered the USA on a B-1 Visa to visit Charleston, SC. She has a visa valid for 10 years, however her I-94/Entry stamp indicates she can only come to the USA for 6 months for this recent trip. While on vacation she meets Uriel, a United States Citizen. It was love at first sight. He proposes to Aileen and they marry after her authorized stay expired and Aileen remains in the USA after her authorized stay expired. If you are filing this case AFTER her stay expired, you should NOT file for Advance Parole Form I-131. If Aileen needs to leave the USA after filing her case, she cannot return to the USA on her Advance Parole.

Mail complete package to USCIS drop box address based on the area your clients reside. Always verify online with USCIS.gov. The

---

2 Overstay Bars: Where one remains in the USA 120 days to less than one year after their authorized stay, they will be subject to the 3 year bar for readmission into the USA after their departure. For persons who remain in the USA for one year or more, they will be subject to the 10 year bar for readmission.

address is subject to change.

Note: Always verify forms, filing fees and address of filing at uscis.gov as they are subject to change. Forms have expiration dates and filing fees and mailing addresses change often. If you do not have an Immigration specific software company that automatically updates forms and send notifications informing you, always go to uscis.gov.

Once you file the case USCIS will mail the I-797 NOTICE OF ACTION receipt notice to the attorney of record and the Petitioner. You will get receipt notices for all forms filed excluding the G-1145, G-325A's, I-864s and Medicals.

You should get your Notice of Action within 30 days from USCIS. The Notice of Action will contain a "Receipt number" of which you may use to check the status of your case online at uscis.gov. It will also contain a telephone number at the bottom of the page for you to contact USCIS to inquire about the case.

The Foreign national will receive a "Biometric" appointment within 30-60 days. This is a Fingerprint appointment where no attorney needs to be present. The client will take their appointment notice to the address provided and follow instructions within the notice. At the Biometrics appointment they will need a valid I.D. They will have their fingerprints and photograph taken for a background check.

All inquiries with USCIS online, in person or by telephone will require:

1. G-28 on record;
2. Petitioner and Beneficiary name and date of birth;
3. Address of Attorney and Clients; and
4. Receipt number

5

The Marriage Interview

All cases filed will require an interview with USCIS officials. An attorney should be present. Both the Petitioning US citizen spouse and the Beneficiary-Foreign national must be present. At the interview, you have the burden of proof to prove it is a "real marriage." You will receive a notice of interview approximately 30 days before your appointment. You must present solid information showing:

- ☐ Your client entered lawfully without dual intent;
- ☐ Your clients are lawfully married;
- ☐ Your clients are in a bona fide marriage;

Note: You must bring all ORIGINAL documents you submitted with the case to the interview. You are permitted to bring any additional/supplemental documentation to the interview. You must bring originals and copies. USCIS officials keep copies and not originals. DO NOT submit originals for USCIS officials to keep as they are unlikely to be returned.

I suggest you bring your clients into the office the week of their interview to prep them. Do a mock interview with your clients. USCIS officials will ask questions that are on the forms filed. It is important that your client know their date of marriage, date of birth of their spouse, their address, how they met and other information a married couple should know.

When you arrive at the interview, arrive no more than 30 minutes prior to your interview. Make sure you leave your cell phone in your car and everyone has government-issued identification so that you can get through security. Attorneys must have your bar card, identification and the appointment letter readily available. After you are checked by security, present your appointment notice to the designated window instructed by the security officer or immigration representative. You must check in for your appointment or they will not know that you are there and they will deny your case for lack of prosecution.

If your client arrives first, advise them to not check-in until you arrive. They may call your clients for interview and proceed without the legal representative. Make sure all parties are present before checking-in.

If you are using an interpreter, they cannot be a party to the case. Many USCIS officials no longer allow Attorneys to translate for their clients. An interpreter may be a family member, friend or translator professional. They must have government issued identification. I suggest they be in the USA legally! They will be required to fill out a Certificate of Translation onsite.

The officer will likely call the name of the beneficiary when it is time for your clients to be interviewed. Do not be alarmed if they decide to interview them separately. Interviewing separately does not mean that two separate officers will interview your clients at the same time. It simply means that while one person is being interviewed the other spouse will wait in the waiting area.

Many times the married couple is interviewed together but it is a decision made by the intervening officer how they want to conduct the interview. Interviews may last anywhere from 30 minutes to two hours.

During the interview, the clients will be sworn in under oath to "tell the truth the whole truth and nothing but the truth" to the officer asking questions. When the officer is ready to proceed with questions, each officer's style varies. Some officers are more aggressive than others. Remain calm and patient and make sure you tell your clients to listen to the questions that are asked before responding.

Some officers do not like when one spouse interrupts and answers questions for the other spouse. Follow the instructions of the officer and they will tell you how they like their interviews to flow. If your client does not understand the question, it is okay to ask the officer to repeat the question. It is always best to clarify so that your client does not give the incorrect answer and it appears to be inconsistencies their statements. Surprisingly enough, many married couples do not remember the date of marriage or their spouse's birthday. If your client does not remember anything else, it is very important that they remember their date of marriage as well as their spouse's birthday.

There aren't any surprises in the interview process. Questions that are asked by the interviewing officer are related to answers that you provided in their applications. On some occasions, the interviewing officer may ask questions about the marriage that are not included in the evidence for the application submitted. Those questions sometimes are related to your client's relationship with in-laws, last vacation together, the engagement, etc. If your clients do not remember exact dates, tell them in advance to try to think of the month and year. Where they cannot remember the exact month or year, try to remember a holiday or special event that occurred around that time. It is natural to forget minor details when nervous. Advise your clients to take their time and think about their response and then respond.

If your application packet was solid and you provide all of the necessary documentation, it is likely that your interview will be closer to the 30 minute mark versus the two hour mark. Interviews that take about two hours or more are usually in cases where the parties are separated. Parties are typically separated in cases where the immigration officer has reviewed the file and subjectively determine that there is a possibility of marriage fraud. It is your burden to prove that your client's marriage is a real marriage and not entered into solely for immigration purposes.

At the end of your marriage interview, the officer may approve your case immediately or tell you they will make a decision. If the case is approved the day of the interview, the officer can stamp the Foreign national's passport with the code that indicates approval (I-551). The Lawful Permanent Resident card will then be mailed to your client from the service center.

In some instances you may be issued an I-72 which is a Request for Additional Evidence, where the officer will ask for additional documentation to prove your bona fide marriage before making a final decision. If you're issued an I- 72, you must provide the requested documents on or before the date noted on your notice. It is best to be over-prepared and provide all of the documents in your client's case before and at the interview to avoid unnecessary delays. If your client's case is approved before their second wedding anniversary, the beneficiary will only get conditional resident status valid for two years.

Many times, clients believe their case is complete at the time they file their case. THEY ARE WRONG! Upon filing the case, clients and attorneys must treat the case as ongoing. Collect all joint documents and evidence on a monthly basis until the day of your interview. If your clients have been married for less than two years you still have to prepare to remove conditional residency.

Keep things organized! You do not want to wait until the last minute to gather six months to two years worth of documentation within 2 to 3 weeks. The burden of proof is on the applicants.

Preparation is key to a successful case and a positive outcome — APPROVAL!

6

Marriage Fraud Allegations

If you have a client who admits to marriage for convenience of obtaining lawful permanent residence, you are participating in fraud. Parties must be in a bona fide marriage. Any marriage entered into for the purpose of obtaining a "green card" is fraud. If USCIS makes an allegation of marriage fraud, defend your clients. To be found to have committed marriage fraud is a bar for future immigration benefits, unless they qualify for a waiver.

The test for fraudulent marriage, also known as a "sham marriage," is did the groom and bride intend to establish a life together when they married? If there is no intent to establish a life together, it is deemed a "sham marriage." As their attorney, it is important to advise your client that USCIS looks at the conduct of the parties before and after the marriage. As mentioned above, the petitioner must present evidence to reflect a real marriage. See checklist from the previous chapter.

As an attorney, you will come across various clients and various situations with marriage based cases. While your clients' may come to you seeking legal assistance and their marriage may not be ideal, such as age differences, language differences, or cultural differences, you have the burden of proof to prove that the marriage was not entered into for the sole purpose of obtaining an immigration benefits.

In the world of social media, everything is recorded. Although USCIS officials are entitled to investigate, investigation of marriage fraud cases must be reasonable. Investigators look at Facebook, Instagram and other social media outlets to determine whether parties are in a real marriage. It is important to advise your client that their case may be investigated by immigration officials. If they are on social media at events without their spouse and out in public in a romantic relationship with someone other than their spouse this can cause an issue.

At the marriage interview if there are inconsistencies of statements this can be a basis for denial as well. If your client does not know their address, does not know their marriage date, does not know where or how they met, etc., these may be fraud indicators for USCIS. Photographs, believe it or not, can lead an adjudicating officer to suspect fraud. Staged photographs are a red flag just as much as intimate photographs that one normally would not share with public.

Remember those affidavits previously mentioned that your clients' friends and family members prepared to support the bona fide marriage? Immigration investigators may contact those persons who wrote those affidavits for additional information and verification. Immigration officials may also interview neighbors where your clients live.

If there is a finding of marriage fraud, immigration officials must provide your client with an opportunity to review all derogatory information. Your clients also have an opportunity to rebut that derogatory information. Immigration officials will send a "Notice of intent to deny," to which you must respond within the time they indicate. There are cases where immigration officials will suspect marriage fraud where there is none. You still must respond and rebut all derogatory information.

As an attorney, your client may not tell you everything and there may be a case where there is marriage fraud and a finding of marriage fraud. Your client may admit to marriage fraud in the interview or in writing by sending in a statement that they were paid by the foreign national in order to obtain lawful permanent resident status. Where there is an admission to marriage fraud and the US citizen petitioner signs an affidavit, in order to avoid prosecution, they also agreed to withdraw the I-130 petition on behalf of the beneficiary. Withdrawing the petition for alien relatives means your foreign national is no longer eligible for lawful permanent residency based on that marriage petition.

It is important to explain marriage fraud to your clients and during every consultation. I suggest that once you are retained, include a clause in your retainer notifying them of the penalties that the clients initial.

While immigration officials can make a finding of marriage fraud to convict a person under this section, the government must prove (1) the person knowingly entered into a marriage; (2) the marriage was entered into for the purpose of circumventing immigration laws; and (3) the person knew or had reason to know that they were violating immigration laws.

Oddly, there may be a client who does not know they are committing marriage fraud. They agree to help out a friend not knowing it is illegal to marry just for the "green card." While ignorance of the law is no excuse, as the attorney I would be sure to cover this in consultation with both spouses.

7

Removing Conditional Residence

If your clients have been married for less than two years at the time the lawful permanent residency is approved, the foreign national's status will only be valid for two years. The lawful permanent resident card will contain a date of expiration, two years from the date of approval. Whether your clients are living together, separated or divorced, Form I-751 Removal of Conditional Residence must be filed. Both spouses must sign this form if they are still married and living together.

It is important to advise your clients that their case continues within two years and they must contact you in time to file the I-751. Form I-751 must be filed with USCIS ninety days before it expires. You should have a tickler system to remind you to contact the clients. This will be a new case and new retainer for your office. I would not make it the attorney's responsibility to contact the clients, however. USCIS does not send reminders to file. I would make it the clients' responsibility to contact the office, but have a tickler in place as a law practice management option.

If filing the I-751 jointly, include additional information that was not provided in your initial filing. Joint documents that reflect a life together and commingling of assets, e.g. bank accounts, auto insurance, life insurance, joint tax returns, etc. You should advise your clients to treat the case as ongoing after initial approval. If they have celebrated holidays, vacations, birthdays take pictures and enclose copies of those events in the evidence. Have your clients write the date of the event on the back of the photos.

When filing to Remove Conditions, include supporting evidence and filing fees with your filing. Always verify the filing fee and filing address online at uscis.gov. Upon filing you will receive a receipt notice from USCIS which will be proof of filing. You will also receive a Notice of Action extending the foreign nationals status for one year while the case is being reviewed and adjudicated. This is helpful to your foreign national client who may need to travel outside the United States. The lawful permanent resident card will have an expiration date. The Notice of Action extending the status for a year is proof of valid and current lawful status in the United States. I always advise my clients to take that notice to a local USCIS office with their lawful permanent resident card and valid passport to obtain a "stamp" in their passport of their pending I-751. Some local offices permit walk-ins and others require an "Infopass" appointment. You can make "Infopass" appointments online at uscis.gov.

Where your I-751 is properly documented and your clients are still living together, the chances of getting the conditions removed without having another interview is stronger. In some cases, your clients may be called in for another interview to prove their marriage is "bona fide." Just like the initial I-130 marriage interview, parties may be interviewed together or separately. Questions will be asked about the marital relationship. Questions may be related to information submitted or information USCIS obtained during their ongoing investigation since the initial approval.

Divorce/Separated Clients Before Conditions are Removed

If your clients are divorced or separated, the foreign national still must file Form I-751. There is a section on Form I-751 that allows one to request to waive the "joint filing requirement." The foreign national is the only person signing this form. If filing separately based on divorce, it is important to enclose a copy of the divorce decree. If you are not the attorney that represented the client in the divorce, make sure you review the divorce decree for any admission of fraud or misrepresentation allegations by the US citizen petitioner. This is a red flag!

If the divorce was based on fraud or misrepresentation related to obtaining the green card, you will have to mitigate/defend these allegations with a brief on this issue. Sometimes the divorce record may be helpful if there was abuse admitted by the US citizen. This will help in proving that the marriage was not entered into by the foreign national to circumvent immigration laws and that the termination was reasonable. Any evidence the foreign national is able to present to prove the "bona fide" marriage (e.g. pictures, children of the marriage, children outside the marriage by the US citizen, joint documents, affidavits from family and friends, etc.) will be beneficial.

Death of the US Citizen spouse

If the US citizen spouse dies before conditional residence is removed, the foreign national still must file FormI-751 and provide all documentation previously mentioned to support a bona fide marriage. They must also enclose the Death Certificate. The Death Certificate must state that the deceased was married and list the name of the living spouse.

Once conditional resident status has been removed your client will receive a new lawful permanent resident card (green card) valid for ten years. Your client can renew the green card every ten years and no longer has to prove a "bona fide" marriage. To renew the green card or replace a lost/stolen green card, your client will need to file Form I-90.

Your client may want to apply for naturalization to become a United States citizen. As a United States citizen, one can vote and receive the same benefits as one born in the United States. If your client obtained their green card based on a marriage based case, they only need to wait three years from the date of the initial approval date to apply. Not three years from the date the conditional residence was removed. Naturalization is a separate subject matter covered in another series.

Appendix

EASY IMMIGRATION PUBLICATIONS

SAMPLE INTAKE

1. Today's Date ______/______/______	2. Your Name (LAST, FIRST)	3. Email:
5. Your Home Phone Number: ( ) ______________	6. Your Mobile Phone Number: ( ) ______________	7. Client Immigration File Number: A______________

Who referred you to our office? ______________________________

Emergency Contact person: ______________________ Telephone: ________________

Address (Street) (Apt.No) ______________________	Employer: ______________________
______________________ (City) (State) (Zip)	______________________ (City) (State) (Zip)
Language spoken: ______________________	Occupation: ______________________

Client's Current Criminal and Immigration History
Are you currently: Court/location (State) (Date) □ In Immigration Proceedings → → → → □ Ever been ordered Deported/Removed → → → → □ Caught at the border or refused admission into the USA → ☞ Next Court date (if any) ________/________/________ Ever been arrested anywhere in the world? Y/N: When? ______________ Where? ______________ Reason?: ______________ Outcome/Disposition: ______________________

Country of Citizenship?	Country of Birth/Date of Birth
______________________	__________/__________

Are you Married? □ **Yes** □ **No** **How many years?** ______ **Immigration status of spouse?** ______________ **Previously Married? Y/N** **How many times?** ______ **Divorced/Widow?**______________ **Location of previous marriage(s)/Divorce?** ______________________
Are you a victim of a crime/domestic violence: Y/N

Sample Intake Form

Do you have any children? □ **Yes** →→→ **How many?** ________ **Immigration status of child(ren) ?**
□ **No**
Age(s): ______________________________ ______________________________

Do you have any other immediate relatives in the USA? □ **Yes** →→→ **Who?** ______________________
Immigration status? □ **No**

Is your Mother or Father a US citizen? □ **Yes** **Which one?** ________________________
□ **No**

□ **By Birth**
□ **Naturalized (date)**__________________

When did you enter the USA? _________/___________/____________

How did you enter the USA?
□ Visa (type)_________________ (I-94 number) ____________________ Stay Expires? _____________
□ Illegally
□ Legally (Border crossing)
□ Asylum

Do you currently have an Immigration lawyer? Y/N	**Do you have a family/criminal lawyer? Y/N**
Name: Telephone: Email:	Name: Telephone: Email:

Immigration History

Date of last entry into USA? ________/________/_____________
Location of entry? ______________________________

Briefly explain your visit here today:

DEPARTMENT OF HOMELAND SECURITY
U.S. Customs and Border Protection

OMB No. 1651-0111

Admission Number

Welcome to the United States

943430429 12

I-94 Arrival/Departure Record - Instructions

This form must be completed by all persons except U.S. Citizens, returning resident aliens, aliens with immigrant visas, and Canadian Citizens visiting or in transit.

Type or print legibly with pen in ALL CAPITAL LETTERS. Use English. Do not write on the back of this form.

This form is in two parts. Please complete both the Arrival Record (Items 1 through 13) and the Departure Record (Items 14 through 17).

When all items are completed, present this form to the CBP Officer.

Item 7 - If you are entering the United States by land, enter **LAND** in this space. If you are entering the United States by ship, enter **SEA** in this space.

CBP Form I-94 (10/04)

Admission Number

OMB No. 1651-0111

943430429 12

Arrival Record

1. Family Name
2. First (Given) Name
3. Birth Date (Day/Mo/Yr)
4. Country of Citizenship
5. Sex (Male or Female)
6. Passport Number
7. Airline and Flight Number
8. Country Where You Live
9. City Where You Boarded
10. City Where Visa Was Issued
11. Date Issued (Day/Mo/Yr)
12. Address While in the United States (Number and Street)
13. City and State

CBP Form I-94 (10/04)

Departure Number

OMB No. 1651-0111

943430429 12

I-94
Departure Record

14. Family Name
15. First (Given) Name
16. Birth Date (Day/Mo/Yr)
17. Country of Citizenship

CBP Form I-94 (10/04)

See Other Side

STAPLE HERE

This Side For Government Use Only

Primary Inspection

Applicant's Name ________

Date Referred ________ Time ________ Insp.# ________

Reason Referred

☐ 212A ☐ PP ☐ Visa ☐ Parole ☐ SLB ☐ TWOV

☐ Other ________

Secondary Inspection

End Secondary Time ________ Insp.# ________

Disposition ________

18. Occupation	19. Waivers
20. CIS A Number A-	21. CIS FCO
22. Petition Number	23. Program Number
24. ☐ Bond	25. ☐ Prospective Student

26. Itinerary/Comments

27. TWOV Ticket Number

Warning - A nonimmigrant who accepts unauthorized employment is subject to deportation.

Important - Retain this permit in your possession; ***you must surrender it when you leave the U.S.*** Failure to do so may delay your entry into the U.S. in the future.
You are authorized to stay in the U.S. only until the date written on this form. To remain past this date, without permission from Department of Homeland Security authorities, is a violation of the law.

Surrender this permit when you leave the U.S.:
- By sea or air, to the transportation line;
- Across the Canadian border, to a Canadian Official;
- Across the Mexican border, to a U.S. Official.

Students planning to reenter the U.S. within 30 days to return to the same school, see "Arrival-Departure" on page 2 of Form I-20 **prior to surrendering this permit.**

Record of Changes

Port: **Departure Record**

Date:

Carrier:

Flight #/Ship Name:

Admission Stamp

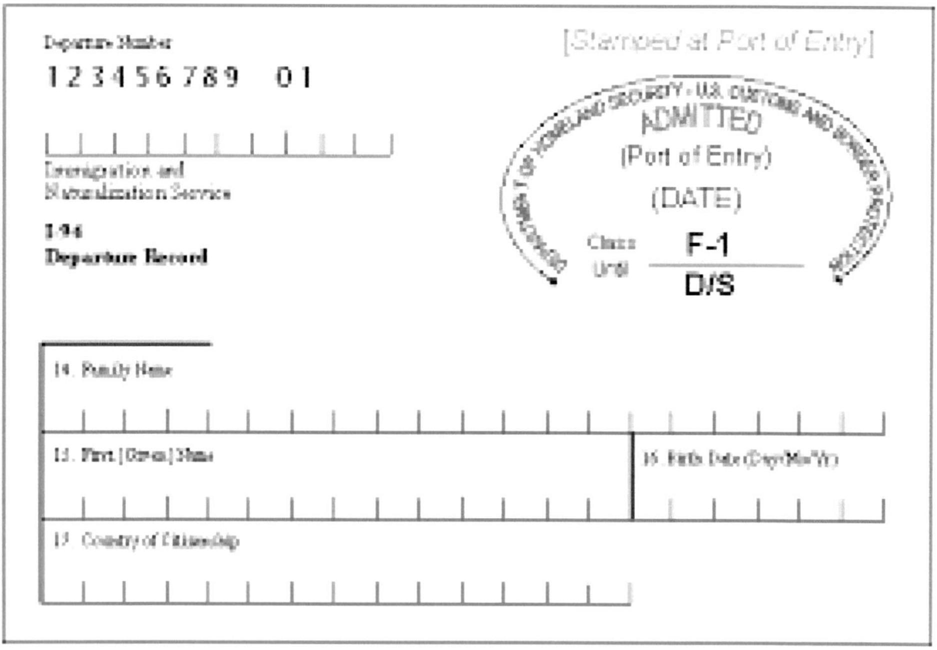
Departure Number
1 2 3 4 5 6 7 8 9   0 1

Immigration and
Naturalization Service

I-94
Departure Record

[Stamped at Port of Entry]

ADMITTED
(Port of Entry)
(DATE)
Class F-1
Until D/S

14. Family Name

15. First (Given) Name

16. Birth Date (Day/Mo/Yr)

17. Country of Citizenship

USCIS Photo Requirements

Please be sure to follow the guidelines as indicated in the following graphic. These are different from the side poses that were required previously. Also, be sure to write (in pencil) your name and admission number on the back of the photos.

The photos must be in color, with a plain background.
All photos must meet size and image specifications.
Photos must be of the applicant only.
When more than one photo is required, all photos of the person must be identical.
The photos must be no more than 30 days old when an application is filed.
The rules regarding head and face coverings have not changed. In general, head and face coverings are not acceptable on immigration photographs. However, the Foreign Affairs Manual (FAM) delineates very limited circumstances (medical or relgious) when such coverings might be acceptable.

Head Position and Placement

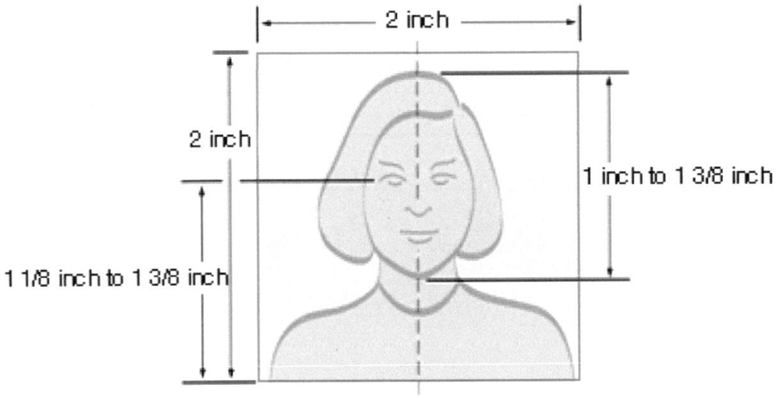

Obsolete ADIT Style Photo
(shown for reference purposes only)

Well Composed Photos

SAMPLE G-1145

e-Notification of Application/Petition Acceptance

Department of Homeland Security
U.S. Citizenship and Immigration Services

USCIS
Form G-1145
OMB No. 1615-0109
Expires 09/30/2016

What Is the Purpose of This Form?

Use this form to request an electronic notification (e-Notification) when U.S. Citizenship and Immigration Services accepts your immigration application. This service is available for applications filed at a USCIS Lockbox facility.

General Information

Complete the information below and clip this form to the first page of your application package. You will receive one e-mail and/or text message for each form you are filing.

We will send the e-Notification within 24 hours after we accept your application. Domestic customers will receive an e-mail and/or text message; overseas customers will only receive an e-mail. Undeliverable e-Notifications cannot be resent.

The e-mail or text message will display your receipt number and tell you how to get updated case status information. It will not include any personal information. The e-Notification does not grant any type of status or benefit; rather it is provided as a convenience to customers.

USCIS will also mail you a receipt notice (I-797C), which you will receive within 10 days after your application has been accepted; use this notice as proof of your pending application or petition.

USCIS Privacy Act Statement

AUTHORITIES: The information requested on this form is collected pursuant to section 103(a) of the Immigration and Nationality Act, as amended INA section 101, et seq.

PURPOSE: The primary purpose for providing the information on this form is to request an electronic notification when USCIS accepts immigration form. The information you provide will be used to send you a text and/or email message.

DISCLOSURE: The information you provide is voluntary. However, failure to provide the requested information may prevent USCIS from providing you a text and/or email message receipting your immigration form.

ROUTINE USES: The information provide on this form will be used by and disclosed to DHS personnel and contractors in accordance with approved routine uses, as described in the associated published system of records notices [**DHS-USCIS-007 - Benefits Information System and DHS-USCIS-001 - Alien File (A-File) and Central Index System (CIS),** which can be found at www.dhs.gov/privacy]. The information may also be made available, as appropriate for law enforcement purposes or in the interest of national security.

Paperwork Reduction Act

An agency may not conduct or sponsor an information collection and a person is not required to respond to a collection of information unless it displays a currently valid OMB control number. The public reporting burden for this collection of information is estimated at 3 minutes per response, including the time for reviewing instructions and completing and submitting the form. Send comments regarding this burden estimate or any other aspect of this collection of information, including suggestions for reducing this burden, to: U.S. Citizenship and Immigration Services, Regulatory Coordination Division, Office of Policy and Strategy, 20 Massachusetts Avenue, NW, Washington, DC 20529-2140. OMB No. 1615-0109. **Do not mail your completed Form G-1145 to this address.**

Complete this form and clip it on top of the first page of your immigration form(s).

Applicant/Petitioner Full Last Name	Applicant/Petitioner Full First Name	Applicant/Petitioner Full Middle Name
E-mail Address		Mobile Phone Number (Text Message)

SAMPLE G-28

Notice of Entry of Appearance as Attorney or Accredited Representative

Department of Homeland Security

DHS
Form G-28
OMB No. 1615-0105
Expires 03/31/2018

Part 1. Information About Attorney or Accredited Representative

1. USCIS ELIS Account Number *(if any)*
▶ [ ]

Name and Address of Attorney or Accredited Representative

2.a. Family Name *(Last Name)* [ ]
2.b. Given Name *(First Name)* [ ]
2.c. Middle Name [ ]
3.a. Street Number and Name [ ]
3.b. Apt. ☐ Ste. ☐ Flr. ☐ [ ]
3.c. City or Town [ ]
3.d. State [ ] 3.e. ZIP Code [ ]
3.f. Province [ ]
3.g. Postal Code [ ]
3.h. Country [ ]
4. Daytime Telephone Number [ ]
5. Fax Number [ ]
6. E-Mail Address *(if any)* [ ]
7. Mobile Telephone Number *(if any)* [ ]

Part 2. Notice of Appearance as Attorney or Accredited Representative

This appearance relates to immigration matters before *(Select **only one** box)*:

1.a. ☐ USCIS
1.b. List the form numbers [ ]
2.a. ☐ ICE
2.b. List the specific matter in which appearance is entered [ ]
3.a. ☐ CBP
3.b. List the specific matter in which appearance is entered [ ]

I enter my appearance as attorney or accredited representative at the request of:

4. Select **only one** box:
☐ Applicant ☐ Petitioner ☐ Requestor
☐ Respondent (ICE, CBP)

Information About Applicant, Petitioner, Requestor, or Respondent

5.a. Family Name *(Last Name)* [ ]
5.b. Given Name *(First Name)* [ ]
5.c. Middle Name [ ]
6. Name of Company or Organization *(if applicable)* [ ]

Part 2. Notice of Appearance as Attorney or Accredited Representative *(continued)*

Information About Applicant, Petitioner, Requestor, or Respondent (continued)

7. USCIS ELIS Account Number *(if any)*

▶

8. Alien Registration Number (A-Number) or Receipt Number

9. Daytime Telephone Number

10. Mobile Telephone Number *(if any)*

11. E-Mail Address *(if any)*

Mailing Address of Applicant, Petitioner, Requestor, or Respondent

NOTE: Provide the mailing address of the applicant, petitioner, requestor, or respondent. If the applicant, petitioner, requestor, or respondent has used a safe mailing address on the application, petition, or request being filed with this Form G-28, provide it in these spaces.

12.a. Street Number and Name

12.b. Apt. ☐ Ste. ☐ Flr. ☐

12.c. City or Town

12.d. State **12.e.** ZIP Code

12.f. Province

12.g. Postal Code

12.h. Country

Part 3. Eligibility Information for Attorney or Accredited Representative

Select **all applicable** items.

1.a. ☐ I am an attorney eligible to practice law in, and a member in good standing of, the bar of the highest courts of the following states, possessions, territories, commonwealths, or the District of Columbia. *(If you need additional space, use **Part 6.**)*

Licensing Authority

1.b. Bar Number *(if applicable)*

1.c. Name of Law Firm

1.d. **I** *(choose one)* ☐ ***am not*** ☐ ***am***

subject to any order of any court or administrative agency disbarring, suspending, enjoining, restraining, or otherwise restricting me in the practice of law. If you are subject to any orders, explain in the space below. *(If you need additional space, use **Part 6**.)*

2.a. ☐ I am an accredited representative of the following qualified nonprofit religious, charitable, social service, or similar organization established in the United States, so recognized by the Department of Justice, Board of Immigration Appeals, in accordance with 8 CFR 292.2. Provide the name of the organization and the expiration date of accreditation.

2.b. Name of Recognized Organization

2.c. Date accreditation expires

(mm/dd/yyyy) ▶

Part 3. Eligibility Information for Attorney or Accredited Representative *(continued)*

3. ☐ I am associated with

________________________________,

the attorney or accredited representative of record who previously filed Form G-28 in this case, and my appearance as an attorney or accredited representative is at his or her request.

NOTE: If you select this item, also complete **Item Numbers 1.a. - 1.b. or Item Numbers 2.a. - 2.c.** in **Part 3.** *(whichever is appropriate).*

4.a. ☐ I am a law student or law graduate working under the direct supervision of the attorney or accredited representative of record on this form in accordance with the requirements in 8 CFR 292.1(a)(2)(iv).

4.b. Name of Law Student or Law Graduate

____

Part 4. Applicant, Petitioner, Requestor, or Respondent Consent to Representation, Contact Information, and Signature

Consent to Representation and Release of Information

1. I have requested the representation of and consented to being represented by the attorney or accredited representative named in **Part 1.** of this form. According to the Privacy Act of 1974 and DHS policy, I also consent to the disclosure to the named attorney or accredited representative of any record pertaining to me that appears in any system of records of USCIS, ICE or CBP.

When you (the applicant, petitioner, requestor, or respondent) are represented, DHS will send notices to both you and your attorney or accredited representative either through mail or electronic delivery.

DHS will also send the Form I-94, Arrival Departure Record, to you **unless** you select **Item Number 2.a.** in **Part 4.** All secure identity documents and Travel Documents will be sent to you (the applicant, petitioner, requestor, or respondent) unless you ask us to send those documents to your attorney of record or accredited representative.

If you do not want to receive original notices or secure identity documents directly, but would rather have such notices and documents sent to your attorney of record or accredited representative, please select **all applicable** boxes below:

2.a ☐ I request DHS send any notice (including Form I-94) on an application, petition, or request to the business address of my attorney of record or accredited representative as listed in this form. I understand that I may change this election at any future date through written notice to DHS.

2.b. ☐ I request that DHS send any secure identity document, such as a Permanent Resident Card, Employment Authorization Document, or Travel Document, that I am approved to receive and authorized to possess, to the business address of my attorney of record or accredited representative as listed in this form. I consent to having my secure identity document sent to my attorney of record or accredited representative and understand that I may request, at any future date and through written notice to DHS, that DHS send any secure identity document to me directly.

3.a. Signature of Applicant, Petitioner, Requestor, or Respondent

➡ ________________________________

3.b. Date of Signature *(mm/dd/yyyy)* ▶ ____________

Part 5. Signature of Attorney or Accredited Representative

I have read and understand the regulations and conditions contained in 8 CFR 103.2 and 292 governing appearances and representation before the Department of Homeland Security. I declare under penalty of perjury under the laws of the United States that the information I have provided on this form is true and correct.

1. Signature of Attorney or Accredited Representative

____

2. Signature of Law Student or Law Graduate

____

3. Date of Signature *(mm/dd/yyyy)* ▶ ____________

Part 6. Additional Information

Use the space below to provide additional information pertaining to **Part 3., Item Numbers 1.a. - 1.d.**

SAMPLE I-130

Department of Homeland Security
U.S. Citizenship and Immigration Services

OMB No. 1615-0012; Expires 12/31/2015

I-130, Petition for Alien Relative

DO NOT WRITE IN THIS BLOCK - FOR USCIS OFFICE ONLY

A#	Action Stamp	Fee Stamp
Section of Law/Visa Category ☐ 201(b) Spouse - IR-1/CR-1 ☐ 201(b) Child - IR-2/CR-2 ☐ 201(b) Parent - IR-5 ☐ 203(a)(1) Unm. S or D - F1-1 ☐ 203(a)(2)(A)Spouse - F2-1 ☐ 203(a)(2)(A) Child - F2-2 ☐ 203(a)(2)(B) Unm. S or D - F2-4 ☐ 203(a)(3) Married S or D - F3-1 ☐ 203(a)(4) Brother/Sister - F4-1		Petition was filed on: ________ (priority date) ☐ Personal Interview ☐ Previously Forwarded ☐ Pet. ☐ Ben. " A" File Reviewed ☐ I-485 Filed Simultaneously ☐ Field Investigation ☐ 204(g) Resolved ☐ 203(a)(2)(A) Resolved ☐ 203(g) Resolved

Remarks:

A. Relationship You are the petitioner. Your relative is the beneficiary.

1. I am filing this petition for my: ☐ Spouse ☐ Parent ☐ Brother/Sister ☐ Child

2. Are you related by adoption? ☐ Yes ☐ No

3. Did you gain permanent residence through adoption? ☐ Yes ☐ No

B. Information about you

1. **Name** (Family name in CAPS) (First) (Middle)

2. **Address** (Number and Street) (Apt. No.)

(Town or City) (State/Country) (Zip/Postal Code)

3. **Place of Birth** (Town or City) (State/Country)

4. **Date of Birth**

5. **Gender** ☐ Male ☐ Female

6. **Marital Status** ☐ Married ☐ Single ☐ Widowed ☐ Divorced

7. **Other Names Used** (including maiden name)

8. **Date and Place of Present Marriage** (if married)

9. **U.S. Social Security Number** (If any)

10. **Alien Registration Number**

11. **Name(s) of Prior Spouse(s)**

12. **Date(s) Marriage(s) Ended**

13. **If you are a U.S. citizen, complete the following:**

My citizenship was acquired through (check one):

☐ Birth in the U.S.

☐ Naturalization. Give certificate number and date and place of issuance.

☐ Parents. Have you obtained a certificate of citizenship in your own name?

☐ Yes. Give certificate number, date and place of issuance. ☐ No

14. **If you are a lawful permanent resident alien, complete the following:**

Date and place of admission for or adjustment to lawful permanent residence and class of admission.

14b. **Did you gain permanent resident status through marriage to a U.S. citizen or lawful permanent resident?**

☐ Yes ☐ No

C. Information about your relative

1. **Name** (Family name in CAPS) (First) (Middle)

2. **Address** (Number and Street) (Apt. No.)

(Town or City) (State/Country) (Zip/Postal Code)

3. **Place of Birth** (Town or City) (State/Country)

4. **Date of Birth**

5. **Gender** ☐ Male ☐ Female

6. **Marital Status** ☐ Married ☐ Single ☐ Widowed ☐ Divorced

7. **Other Names Used** (including maiden name)

8. **Date and Place of Present Marriage** (if married)

9. **U.S. Social Security Number** (If any)

10. **Alien Registration Number**

11. **Name(s) of Prior Spouse(s)**

12. **Date(s) Marriage(s) Ended**

13. **Has your relative ever been in the U.S.?** ☐ Yes ☐ No

14. **If your relative is currently in the U.S., complete the following:**

He or she arrived as a:

(visitor, student, stowaway, without inspection, etc.)

Arrival/Departure Record (I-94) **Date arrived**

Date authorized stay expired, or will expire, as shown on Form I-94 or I-95

15. **Name and address of present employer** (if any)

Date this employment began

16. **Has your relative ever been under immigration proceedings?**

☐ No ☐ Yes Where ________ When ________

☐ Removal ☐ Exclusion/Deportation ☐ Rescission ☐ Judicial Proceedings

INITIAL RECEIPT ____ RESUBMITTED ____ RELOCATED: Rec'd ____ Sent ____ COMPLETED: Appv'd ____ Denied ____ Ret'd ____

C. Information about your relative (continued)

17. List spouse and all children of your relative.

(Name) (Relationship) (Date of Birth) (Country of Birth)

18. Address in the United States where your relative intends to live.

(Street Address) (Town or City) (State)

19. Your relative's address abroad. (Include street, city, province and country) Phone Number (if any)

20. If your relative's native alphabet is other than Roman letters, write his or her name and foreign address in the native alphabet.

(Name) Address (Include street, city, province and country):

21. If filing for your spouse, give last address at which you lived together. (Include street, city, province, if any, and country):

From: **To:**

22. Complete the information below if your relative is in the United States and will apply for adjustment of status.

Your relative is in the United States and will apply for adjustment of status to that of a lawful permanent resident at the USCIS office in:

If your relative is not eligible for adjustment of status, he or she will apply for a visa abroad at the American consular post in:

(City) (State) (City) (Country

NOTE: Designation of a U.S. embassy or consulate outside the country of your relative's last residence does not guarantee acceptance for processing by that post. Acceptance is at the discretion of the designated embassy or consulate.

D. Other information

1. If separate petitions are also being submitted for other relatives, give names of each and relationship.

2. Have you ever before filed a petition for this or any other alien? ☐ Yes ☐ No

If "Yes," give name, place and date of filing and result.

WARNING: USCIS investigates claimed relationships and verifies the validity of documents. USCIS seeks criminal prosecutions when family relationships are falsified to obtain visas.

PENALTIES: By law, you may be imprisoned for not more than five years or fined $250,000, or both, for entering into a marriage contract for the purpose of evading any provision of the immigration laws. In addition, you may be fined up to $10,000 and imprisoned for up to five years, or both, for knowingly and willfully falsifying or concealing a material fact or using any false document in submitting this petition.

YOUR CERTIFICATION: I certify, under penalty of perjury under the laws of the United States of America, that the foregoing is true and correct. Furthermore, I authorize the release of any information from my records that U.S. Citizenship and Immigration Services needs to determine eligiblity for the benefit that I am seeking.

E. Signature of petitioner

Date Phone Number ( )

F. Signature of person preparing this form, if other than the petitioner

I declare that I prepared this document at the request of the person above and that it is based on all information of which I have any knowledge.

Print Name ______ Signature ______ Date ______

Address ______ **G-28 ID or VOLAG Number, if any.** ______

SAMPLE G-325A

Department of Homeland Security
U.S. Citizenship and Immigration Services

OMB No. 1615-0008; Expires 06/30/2017

G-325A, Biographic Information

Family Name	First Name	Middle Name	☐ Male ☐ Female	Date of Birth *(mm/dd/yyyy)*	Citizenship/Nationality	File Number A

All Other Names Used (include names by previous marriages)	City and Country of Birth	U.S. Social Security No. *(if any)*

Family Name	First Name	Date of Birth *(mm/dd/yyyy)*	City, and Country of Birth *(if known)*	City and Country of Residence
Father				
Mother (Maiden Name)				

Current Husband or Wife (If none, so state) Family Name (For wife, give maiden name)	First Name	Date of Birth *(mm/dd/yyyy)*	City and Country of Birth	Date of Marriage	Place of Marriage

Former Husbands or Wives (If none, so state) Family Name (For wife, give maiden name)	First Name	Date of Birth *(mm/dd/yyyy)*	Date and Place of Marriage	Date and Place of Termination of Marriage

Applicant's residence last five years. List present address first.

Street Name and Number	City	Province or State	Country	From Month	Year	To Month	Year
						Present Time	

Applicant's last address outside the United States of more than 1 year.

Street Name and Number	City	Province or State	Country	From Month	Year	To Month	Year

Applicant's employment last five years. (If none, so state.) List present employment first.

Full Name and Address of Employer	Occupation (Specify)	From Month	Year	To Month	Year
				Present Time	

Last occupation abroad if not shown above. (Include all information requested above.)

This form is submitted in connection with an application for:	**Signature of Applicant**	**Date**
☐ Naturalization ☐ Other (Specify): ☐ Status as Permanent Resident	➡	

If your native alphabet is in other than Roman letters, write your name in your native alphabet below:

Penalties: Severe penalties are provided by law for knowingly and willfully falsifying or concealing a material fact.

Applicant: **Print your name and Alien Registration Number in the box outlined by heavy border below.**

Complete This Box (Family Name)	**(Given Name)**	**(Middle Name)**	**(Alien Registration Number)**
			A

Form G-325A (Rev. 06/01/15) Y

Instructions

What Is the Purpose of This Form?

USCIS will use the information you provide on this form to process your application or petition.

Complete this biographical information form and include it with the application or petition you are submitting to U.S. Citizenship and Immigration Services (USCIS).

If you have any questions on how to complete the form, call our National Customer Service Center at **1-800-375-5283**. For TDD (hearing impaired) call: **1-800-767-1833**.

Privacy Act Notice

We ask for the information on this form, and associated evidence, to determine if you have established eligibility for the immigration benefit for which you are filing. Our legal right to ask for this information can be found in the Immigration and Nationality Act, as amended. We may provide this information to other government agencies. Failure to provide this information, and any requested evidence, may delay a final decision or result in denial of your immigration benefit.

Paperwork Reduction Act

An agency may not conduct or sponsor an information collection and a person is not required to respond to a collection of information unless it displays a currently valid OMB control number. The public reporting burden for this collection of information is estimated at 15 minutes per response, including the time for reviewing instructions and completing and submitting the form. Send comments regarding this burden estimate or any other aspect of this collection of information, including suggestions for reducing this burden, to: U.S. Citizenship and Immigration Services, Regulatory Coordination Division, Office of Policy and Strategy, 20 Massachusetts Avenue, NW, Washington, DC 20529-2140, OMB No. 1615-0008. **Do not mail your completed Form G-325A to this address.**

SAMPLE I-485

OMB No. 1615-0023; Expires 10/31/17

Department of Homeland Security
U.S. Citizenship and Immigration Services

Form I-485, Application to Register Permanent Residence or Adjust Status

START HERE - Type or Print (Use black ink)

Part 1. Information About You

Family Name *(Last Name)* | Given Name *(First Name)* | Middle Name

Address - Street Number and Name | Apt. No.

C/O *(in care of)*

City | State | ZIP Code

Date of Birth *(mm/dd/yyyy)* | Country of Birth

Country of Citizenship/Nationality | U.S. Social Security No. *(if any)* | A-Number *(if any)*

Date of Last Arrival *(mm/dd/yyyy)* | I-94 Arrival-Departure Record Number

Current USCIS Status | Expires on *(mm/dd/yyyy)*

Part 2. Application Type *(Select one)*

I am applying for an adjustment to permanent resident status because:

a. ☐ An immigrant petition giving me an immediately available immigrant visa number that has been approved. (Attach a copy of the approval notice, or a relative, special immigrant juvenile, or special immigrant military visa petition filed with this application that will give you an immediately available visa number, if approved.)

b. ☐ My spouse or parent applied for adjustment of status or was granted lawful permanent residence in an immigrant visa category that allows derivative status for spouses and children.

c. ☐ I entered as a K-1 fiancé(e) of a U.S. citizen whom I married within 90 days of entry, or I am the K-2 child of such a fiancé(e). (Attach a copy of the fiancé(e) petition approval notice and the marriage certificate.)

d. ☐ I was granted asylum or derivative asylum status as the spouse or child of a person granted asylum and am eligible for adjustment.

e. ☐ I am a native or citizen of Cuba admitted or paroled into the United States after January 1, 1959, and thereafter have been physically present in the United States for at least 1 year.

f. ☐ I am the husband, wife, or minor unmarried child of a Cuban described above in **(e),** and I am residing with that person, and was admitted or paroled into the United States after January 1, 1959, and thereafter have been physically present in the United States for at least 1 year.

g. ☐ I have continuously resided in the United States since before January 1, 1972.

h. ☐ Other basis of eligibility. Explain (for example, I was admitted as a refugee, my status has not been terminated, and I have been physically present in the United States for 1 year after admission). If additional space is needed, see **Page 3** of the instructions. ____________

I am already a permanent resident and am applying to have the date I was granted permanent residence adjusted to the date I originally arrived in the United States as a nonimmigrant or parolee, or as of May 2, 1964, whichever date is later, and: *(Select one)*

i. ☐ I am a native or citizen of Cuba and meet the description in **(e)** above.

j. ☐ I am the husband, wife, or minor unmarried child of a Cuban and meet the description in **(f)** above.

For USCIS Use Only

Returned | Receipt

Resubmitted

Reloc Sent

Reloc Rec'd

Applicant Interviewed

Section of Law

☐ Sec. 209(a), INA
☐ Sec. 209(b), INA
☐ Sec. 13, Act of 9/11/57
☐ Sec. 245, INA
☐ Sec. 249, INA
☐ Sec. 1 Act of 11/2/66
☐ Sec. 2 Act of 11/2/66
☐ Other ____________

Country Chargeable

Eligibility Under Sec. 245

☐ Approved Visa Petition
☐ Dependent of Principal Alien
☐ Special Immigrant
☐ Other ____________

Preference

Action Block

To be Completed by
***Attorney or Representative*, if any**

☐ Fill in box if Form G-28 is attached to represent the applicant.

VOLAG No

ATTY State License Number

Form I-485 (Rev. 10/05/15) Y

Part 3. Processing Information

A. City/Town/Village of Birth

Current Occupation

Your Mother's First Name

Your Father's First Name

Provide your name exactly as it appears on your Form I-94, Arrival-Departure Record Number

Place of Last Entry Into the United States *(City/State)*

In what status did you last enter? *(Visitor, student, exchange visitor, crewman, temporary worker, without inspection, etc.)*

Were you inspected by a U.S. Immigration Officer? Yes ☐ No ☐

Nonimmigrant Visa Number

Consulate Where Visa Was Issued

Date Visa Issued *(mm/dd/yyyy)*

Gender ☐ Male ☐ Female

Marital Status ☐ Married ☐ Single ☐ Divorced ☐ Widowed

Have you ever applied for permanent resident status in the U.S.? ☐ Yes *(If "Yes" give date and place of filing and final disposition.)* ☐ No

B. List your present spouse and all of your children (include adult sons and daughters). (If you have none, write "None." If additional space is needed, see **Page 3** of the instructions.)

Family Name *(Last Name)*	Given Name *(First Name)*		Middle Initial	Date of Birth *(mm/dd/yyyy)*
Country of Birth	Relationship	A-Number *(if any)*		Applying with you?
				Yes ☐ No ☐
Family Name *(Last Name)*	Given Name *(First Name)*		Middle Initial	Date of Birth *(mm/dd/yyyy)*
Country of Birth	Relationship	A-Number *(if any)*		Applying with you?
				Yes ☐ No ☐
Family Name *(Last Name)*	Given Name *(First Name)*		Middle Initial	Date of Birth *(mm/dd/yyyy)*
Country of Birth	Relationship	A-Number *(if any)*		Applying with you?
				Yes ☐ No ☐
Family Name *(Last Name)*	Given Name *(First Name)*		Middle Initial	Date of Birth *(mm/dd/yyyy)*
Country of Birth	Relationship	A-Number *(if any)*		Applying with you?
				Yes ☐ No ☐
Family Name *(Last Name)*	Given Name *(First Name)*		Middle Initial	Date of Birth *(mm/dd/yyyy)*
Country of Birth	Relationship	A-Number *(if any)*		Applying with you?
				Yes ☐ No ☐

Part 3. Processing Information *(Continued)*

C. List your present and past membership in or affiliation with every organization, association, fund, foundation, party, club, society, or similar group in the United States or in other places since your 16th birthday. Include **any military service** in this part. If none, write "None." Include the name of each organization, location, nature, and dates of membership. If additional space is needed, attach a separate sheet of paper. Continuation pages must be submitted according to the guidelines provided on **Page 3** of the instructions under **General Instructions**.

Name of Organization	Location and Nature	Date of Membership From	Date of Membership To

Answer the following questions. (If your answer is **"Yes"** to any question, explain on a separate piece of paper. Continuation pages must be submitted according to the guidelines provided on **Page 3** of the instructions under **General Instructions**. Information about documentation that must be included with your application is also provided in this section.) Answering **"Yes"** does not necessarily mean that you are not entitled to adjust status or register for permanent residence.

1. Have you **EVER**, in or outside the United States:

- **a.** Knowingly committed any crime of moral turpitude or a drug-related offense for which you have not been arrested? Yes ☐ No ☐
- **b.** Been arrested, cited, charged, indicted, convicted, fined, or imprisoned for breaking or violating any law or ordinance, excluding traffic violations? Yes ☐ No ☐
- **c.** Been the beneficiary of a pardon, amnesty, rehabilitation decree, other act of clemency, or similar action? Yes ☐ No ☐
- **d.** Exercised diplomatic immunity to avoid prosecution for a criminal offense in the United States? Yes ☐ No ☐

2. Have you received public assistance in the United States from any source, including the U.S. Government or any State, county, city, or municipality (other than emergency medical treatment), or are you likely to receive public assistance in the future? Yes ☐ No ☐

3. Have you **EVER**:

- **a.** Within the past 10 years been a prostitute or procured anyone for prostitution, or intend to engage in such activities in the future? Yes ☐ No ☐
- **b.** Engaged in any unlawful commercialized vice, including, but not limited to, illegal gambling? Yes ☐ No ☐
- **c.** Knowingly encouraged, induced, assisted, abetted, or aided any alien to try to enter the United States illegally? Yes ☐ No ☐
- **d.** Illicitly trafficked in any controlled substance, or knowingly assisted, abetted, or colluded in the illicit trafficking of any controlled substance? Yes ☐ No ☐

4. Have you **EVER** engaged in, conspired to engage in, or do you intend to engage in, or have you ever solicited membership or funds for, or have you through any means ever assisted or provided any type of material support to any person or organization that has ever engaged or conspired to engage in sabotage, kidnapping, political assassination, hijacking, or any other form of terrorist activity? Yes ☐ No ☐

Part 3. Processing Information *(Continued)*

5. Do you intend to engage in the United States in:
   - a. Espionage? Yes ☐ No ☐
   - b. Any activity a purpose of which is opposition to, or the control or overthrow of, the Government of the United States, by force, violence, or other unlawful means? Yes ☐ No ☐
   - c. Any activity to violate or evade any law prohibiting the export from the United States of goods, technology, or sensitive information? Yes ☐ No ☐

6. Have you **EVER** been a member of, or in any way affiliated with, the Communist Party or any other totalitarian party? Yes ☐ No ☐

7. Did you, during the period from March 23, 1933 to May 8, 1945, in association with either the Nazi Government of Germany or any organization or government associated or allied with the Nazi Government of Germany, ever order, incite, assist, or otherwise participate in the persecution of any person because of race, religion, national origin, or political opinion? Yes ☐ No ☐

8. Have you **EVER** been deported from the United States, or removed from the United States at government expense, excluded within the past year, or are you now in exclusion, deportation, removal, or rescission proceedings? Yes ☐ No ☐

9. Are you under a final order of civil penalty for violating section 274C of the Immigration and Nationality Act (INA) for use of fraudulent documents or have you, by fraud or willful misrepresentation of a material fact, ever sought to procure, or procured, a visa, other documentation, entry into the United States, or any immigration benefit? Yes ☐ No ☐

10. Have you **EVER** left the United States to avoid being drafted into the U.S. Armed Forces? Yes ☐ No ☐

11. Have you **EVER** been a J nonimmigrant exchange visitor who was subject to the 2-year foreign residence requirement and have not yet complied with that requirement or obtained a waiver? Yes ☐ No ☐

12. Are you now withholding custody of a U.S. citizen child outside the United States from a person granted custody of the child? Yes ☐ No ☐

13. Do you plan to practice polygamy in the United States? Yes ☐ No ☐

14. Have you **EVER** ordered, incited, called for, committed, assisted, helped with, or otherwise participated in any of the following:
   - a. Acts involving torture or genocide? Yes ☐ No ☐
   - b. Killing any person? Yes ☐ No ☐
   - c. Intentionally and severely injuring any person? Yes ☐ No ☐
   - d. Engaging in any kind of sexual contact or relations with any person who was being forced or threatened? Yes ☐ No ☐
   - e. Limiting or denying any person's ability to exercise religious beliefs? Yes ☐ No ☐

15. Have you **EVER**:
   - a. Served in, been a member of, assisted in, or participated in any military unit, paramilitary unit, police unit, self-defense unit, vigilante unit, rebel group, guerrilla group, militia, or insurgent organization? Yes ☐ No ☐
   - b. Served in any prison, jail, prison camp, detention facility, labor camp, or any other situation that involved detaining persons? Yes ☐ No ☐

16. Have you **EVER** been a member of, assisted in, or participated in any group, unit, or organization of any kind in which you or other persons used any type of weapon against any person or threatened to do so? Yes ☐ No ☐

Part 3. Processing Information *(Continued)*

17. Have you **EVER** assisted or participated in selling or providing weapons to any person who to your knowledge used them against another person, or in transporting weapons to any person who to your knowledge used them against another person? Yes ☐ No ☐

18. Have you **EVER** received any type of military, paramilitary, or weapons training? Yes ☐ No ☐

Part 4. Accommodations for Individuals With Disabilities and/or Impairments *(See **Page** 7 of the instructions before completing this section.)*

Are you requesting an accommodation because of your disability(ies) and/or impairment(s)? Yes ☐ No ☐

If you answered "Yes," select any applicable box:

☐ **a.** I am deaf or hard of hearing and request the following accommodation(s) (if requesting a sign-language interpreter, indicate which language (e.g., American Sign Language)):

☐ **b.** I am blind or sight-impaired and request the following accommodation(s):

☐ **c.** I have another type of disability and/or impairment (describe the nature of your disability(ies) and/or impairment(s) and accommodation(s) you are requesting):

Part 5. Signature *(Read the information on penalties on **Page 8** of the instructions before completing this section. You must file this application while in the United States.)*

Your Registration With U.S. Citizenship and Immigration Services

"I understand and acknowledge that, under section 262 of the Immigration and Nationality Act (INA), as an alien who has been or will be in the United States for more than 30 days, I am required to register with U.S. Citizenship and Immigration Services (USCIS). I understand and acknowledge that, under section 265 of the INA, I am required to provide USCIS with my current address and written notice of any change of address within **10** days of the change. I understand and acknowledge that USCIS will use the most recent address that I provide to USCIS, on any form containing these acknowledgements, for all purposes, including the service of a Notice to Appear should it be necessary for USCIS to initiate removal proceedings against me. I understand and acknowledge that if I change my address without providing written notice to USCIS, I will be held responsible for any communications sent to me at the most recent address that I provided to USCIS. I further understand and acknowledge that, if removal proceedings are initiated against me and I fail to attend any hearing, including an initial hearing based on service of the Notice to Appear at the most recent address that I provided to USCIS or as otherwise provided by law, I may be ordered removed in my absence, arrested, and removed from the United States."

Selective Service Registration

The following applies to you if you are a male at least 18 years of age, but not yet 26 years of age, who is required to register with the Selective Service System: "I understand that my filing Form I-485 with U.S. Citizenship and Immigration Services (USCIS) authorizes USCIS to provide certain registration information to the Selective Service System in accordance with the Military Selective Service Act. Upon USCIS acceptance of my application, I authorize USCIS to transmit to the Selective Service System my name, current address, Social Security Number, date of birth, and the date I filed the application for the purpose of recording my Selective Service registration as of the filing date. If, however, USCIS does not accept my application, I further understand that, if so required, I am responsible for registering with the Selective Service by other means, provided I have not yet reached 26 years of age."

Part 5. Signature *(Continued)*

Applicant's Statement *(Select one)*

☐ I can read and understand English, and I have read and understand each and every question and instruction on this form, as well as my answer to each question.

☐ Each and every question and instruction on this form, as well as my answer to each question, has been read to me in the ________________ language, a language in which I am fluent, by the person named in **Interpreter's Statement and Signature**. I understand each and every question and instruction on this form, as well as my answer to each question.

I certify, under penalty of perjury under the laws of the United States of America, that the information provided with this application is all true and correct. I certify also that I have not withheld any information that would affect the outcome of this application.

I authorize the release of any information from my records that U.S. Citizenship and Immigration Services (USCIS) needs to determine eligibility for the benefit I am seeking.

Signature *(Applicant)*	Print Your Full Name	Date *(mm/dd/yyyy)*	Daytime Phone Number *(include area code)*

NOTE: *If you do not completely fill out this form or fail to submit required documents listed in the instructions, you may not be found eligible for the requested benefit, and this application may be denied.*

Interpreter's Statement and Signature

I certify that I am fluent in English and the below-mentioned language.

Language Used *(language in which applicant is fluent)*

I further certify that I have read each and every question and instruction on this form, as well as the answer to each question, to this applicant in the above-mentioned language, and the applicant has understood each and every instruction and question on the form, as well as the answer to each question.

Signature *(Interpreter)*	Print Your Full Name	Date *(mm/dd/yyyy)*	Daytime Phone Number *(include area code)*

Part 6. Signature of Person Preparing Form, If Other Than Above

I declare that I prepared this application at the request of the above applicant, and it is based on all information of which I have knowledge.

Signature	Print Your Full Name	Date *(mm/dd/yyyy)*	Daytime Phone Number *(include area code)*

Firm Name and Address	Email Address *(if any)*

SAMPLE I-765

OMB No. 1615-0040; Expires 02/28/2018

Department of Homeland Security
U.S. Citizenship and Immigration Services

I-765, Application For Employment Authorization

For USCIS Use Only	Fee Stamp	Action Block	Initial Receipt	Resubmitted
			Relocated	
			Received	Sent
			Completed	
☐ Application Approved ☐ Authorization/Extension Valid From ______ ☐ Authorization/Extension Valid To ______		☐ Application Denied - Failed to establish: ☐ Eligibility under 8 CFR 274a.12 (a) or (c) ☐ Economic necessity under 8 CFR 274a.12(c)(14), (18) and 8 CFR 214.2(f)	Approved	Denied
			A#	
Subject to the following conditions: ______			☐ Applicant is filing under section 274a.12 ______	

I am applying for: ☐ Permission to accept employment. ☐ Replacement (of lost employment authorization document).
☐ Renewal of my permission to accept employment (attach a copy of your previous employment authorization document).

1. **Full Name**
(Family Name) (First Name) (Middle Name)

2. **Other Names Used** (include Maiden Name)

3. **U.S. Mailing Address**
(Street Number and Name) (Apt. Number)
(Town or City) (State) (ZIP Code)

4. **Country of Citizenship or Nationality**

5. **Place of Birth**
(Town or City) (State/Province) (Country)

6. **Date of Birth** (mm/dd/yyyy)

7. **Gender** ☐ Male ☐ Female

8. **Marital Status**
☐ Married ☐ Single ☐ Divorced ☐ Widowed

9. **Social Security Number** (Include all numbers you have ever used, if any)

10. **Alien Registration Number (A-Number)** or **Form I-94 Number** (if any)

11. **Have you ever before applied for employment authorization from USCIS?**
☐ Yes (Complete the following questions.)
Which USCIS Office? Dates
Results (Granted or Denied - attach all documentation)
☐ No (Proceed to **Question 12.**)

12. **Date of Last Entry into the U.S., on or about** (mm/dd/yyyy)

13. **Place of Last Entry into the U.S.**

14. **Status at Last Entry** (B-2 Visitor, F-1 Student, No Lawful Status, etc.)

15. **Current Immigration Status** (Visitor, Student, etc.)

16. **Eligibility Category.** Go to the "**Who May File Form I-765?**" section of the Instructions. In the space below, place the letter and number of the eligibility category you selected from the instructions. For example, (a)(8), (c)(17)(iii), etc.
( ) ( ) ( )

17. **(c)(3)(C) Eligibility Category.** If you entered the eligibility category (c)(3)(C) in **Question 16** above, list your degree, your employer's name as listed in E-Verify, and your employer's E-Verify Company Identification Number or a valid E-Verify Client Company Identification Number in the space below.
Degree Employer's Name as listed in E-Verify
Employer's E-Verify Company Identification Number or a Valid E-Verify Client Company Identification Number

18. **(c)(26) Eligibility Category.** If you entered the eligibility category (c)(26) in **Question 16** above, please provide the receipt number of your H-1B principal spouse's most recent Form I-797 Notice of Approval for Form I-129.

Certification

I certify, under penalty of perjury, that the foregoing is true and correct. Furthermore, I authorize the release of any information that U.S. Citizenship and Immigration Services needs to determine eligibility for the benefit I am seeking. I have read the "**Who May File Form I-765?**" section of the instructions and have identified the appropriate eligibility category in **Question 16**.

Applicant's Signature ______

Date of Signature (mm/dd/yyyy) ______

Telephone Number ______

Signature of Person Preparing Form, If Other Than Applicant

I declare that this document was prepared by me at the request of the applicant and is based on all information of which I have any knowledge.

Preparer's Signature ______

Date of Signature (mm/dd/yyyy) ______

Printed Name ______

Address ______

Form I-765 11/04/15 Y

SAMPLE I-131

Application for Travel Document

Department of Homeland Security
U.S. Citizenship and Immigration Services

USCIS
Form I-131
OMB No. 1615-0013
Expires 03/31/2016

For USCIS Use Only	Receipt	Action Block	To Be Completed by an *Attorney/ Representative*, if any.
	☐ **Document Hand Delivered** By: ______ Date: __/__/__		☐ Fill in box if G-28 is attached to represent the applicant.
	Document Issued ☐ Re-entry Permit *(Update "Mail To" Section)* ☐ Refugee Travel Document *(Update "Mail To" Section)* ☐ Single Advance Parole ☐ Multiple Advance Parole *Valid Until:* __/__/__	**Mail To** *(Re-entry & Refugee Only)* ☐ Address in *Part 1* ☐ US Consulate at: ______ ☐ Intl DHS Ofc at: ______	Attorney State License Number: ______

▶ **Start Here.** Type or Print in Black Ink

Part 1. Information About You

1.a. Family Name *(Last Name)*

1.b. Given Name *(First Name)*

1.c. Middle Name

Physical Address

2.a. In Care of Name

2.b. Street Number and Name

2.c. Apt. ☐ Ste. ☐ Flr ☐

2.d. City or Town

2.e. State **2.f.** Zip Code

2.g. Postal Code

2.h. Province

2.i. Country

Other Information

3. Alien Registration Number (A-Number)

▶ **A-**

4. Country of Birth

5. Country of Citizenship

6. Class of Admission

7. Gender ☐ Male ☐ Female

8. Date of Birth *(mm/dd/yyyy)* ▶

9. U.S. Social Security Number *(if any)*

▶

Part 2. Application Type

1.a. ☐ I am a permanent resident or conditional resident of the United States, and I am applying for a reentry permit.

1.b. ☐ I now hold U.S. refugee or asylee status, and I am applying for a Refugee Travel Document.

1.c. ☐ I am a permanent resident as a direct result of refugee or asylee status, and I am applying for a Refugee Travel Document.

1.d. ☐ I am applying for an Advance Parole Document to allow me to return to the United States after temporary foreign travel.

1.e. ☐ I am outside the United States, and I am applying for an Advance Parole Document.

1.f. ☐ I am applying for an Advance Parole Document for a person who is outside the United States.

If you checked box "1.f." provide the following information about that person in 2.a. through 2.p.

2.a. Family Name *(Last Name)*

2.b. Given Name *(First Name)*

2.c. Middle Name

2.d. Date of Birth *(mm/dd/yyyy)* ▶

2.e. Country of Birth

2.f. Country of Citizenship

2.g. Daytime Phone Number ( ) -

Physical Address (If you checked box 1.f.)

2.h. In Care of Name

2.i. Street Number and Name

2.j. Apt. ☐ Ste. ☐ Flr. ☐

2.k. City or Town

2.l. State 2.m. Zip Code

2.n. Postal Code

2.o. Province

2.p. Country

Part 3. Processing Information

1. Date of Intended Departure *(mm/dd/yyyy)* ▶

2. Expected Length of Trip *(in days)*

3.a. Are you, or any person included in this application, now in exclusion, deportation, removal, or rescission proceedings? ☐ Yes ☐ No

3.b. If "Yes", Name of DHS office:

4.a. Have you ever before been issued a reentry permit or Refugee Travel Document? *(If "Yes" give the following information for the last document issued to you):* ☐ Yes ☐ No

4.b. Date Issued *(mm/dd/yyyy)* ▶

4.c. Disposition *(attached, lost, etc.)*:

If you are applying for a non-DACA related Advance Parole Document, skip to Part 7; ***DACA recipients must complete Part 4 before skipping to Part 7.***

Part 3. Processing Information *(continued)*

Where do you want this travel document sent? *(Check one)*

5. ☐ To the U.S. address shown in **Part 1 (2.a through 2.i.)** of this form.

6. ☐ To a U.S. Embassy or consulate at:

6.a. City or Town

6.b. Country

7. ☐ To a DHS office overseas at:

7.a. City or Town

7.b. Country

If you checked "6" or "7", where should the notice to pick up the travel document be sent?

8. ☐ To the address shown in **Part 2 (2.h. through 2.p.)** of this form.

9. ☐ To the address shown in **Part 3 (10.a. through 10.i.)** of this form.:

10.a. In Care of Name

10.b. Street Number and Name

10.c. Apt. ☐ Ste. ☐ Flr. ☐

10.d. City or Town

10.e. State **10.f.** Zip Code

10.g. Postal Code

10.h. Province

10.i. Country

10.j. Daytime Phone Number ( ) -

Part 4. Information About Your Proposed Travel

1.a. Purpose of trip. *(If you need more space, continue on a separate sheet of paper.)*

1.b. List the countries you intend to visit. *(If you need more space, continue on a separate sheet of paper.)*

Part 5. Complete Only If Applying for a Re-entry Permit

Since becoming a permanent resident of the United States (or during the past 5 years, whichever is less) how much total time have you spent outside the United States?

1.a. ☐ less than 6 months **1.d.** ☐ 2 to 3 years
1.b. ☐ 6 months to 1 year **1.e.** ☐ 3 to 4 years
1.c. ☐ 1 to 2 years **1.f.** ☐ more than 4 years

2. Since you became a permanent resident of the United States, have you ever filed a Federal income tax return as a nonresident or failed to file a Federal income tax return because you considered yourself to be a nonresident? *(If "Yes" give details on a separate sheet of paper.)*

☐ Yes ☐ No

Part 6. Complete Only If Applying for a Refugee Travel Document

1. Country from which you are a refugee or asylee:

If you answer "Yes" to any of the following questions, you must explain on a separate sheet of paper. Include your Name and A-Number on the top of each sheet.

2. Do you plan to travel to the country named above? ☐ Yes ☐ No

Since you were accorded refugee/asylee status, have you ever:

3.a. Returned to the country named above? ☐ Yes ☐ No

3.b. Applied for and/or obtained a national passport, passport renewal, or entry permit of that country? ☐ Yes ☐ No

3.c. Applied for and/or received any benefit from such country (for example, health insurance benefits)? ☐ Yes ☐ No

Since you were accorded refugee/asylee status, have you, by any legal procedure or voluntary act:

4.a. Reacquired the nationality of the country named above? ☐ Yes ☐ No

4.b. Acquired a new nationality? ☐ Yes ☐ No

4.c. Been granted refugee or asylee status in any other country? ☐ Yes ☐ No

Part 7. Complete Only If Applying for Advance Parole

On a separate sheet of paper, explain how you qualify for an Advance Parole Document, and what circumstances warrant issuance of advance parole. Include copies of any documents you wish considered. *(See instructions.)*

1. How many trips do you intend to use this document?

☐ One Trip ☐ More than one trip

If the person intended to receive an Advance Parole Document is outside the United States, provide the location (City or Town and Country) of the U.S. Embassy or consulate or the DHS overseas office that you want us to notify.

2.a. City or Town

2.b. Country

If the travel document will be delivered to an overseas office, where should the notice to pick up the document be sent?:

3. ☐ To the address shown in **Part 2 (2.h. through 2.p.)** of this form.

4. ☐ To the address shown in **Part 7 (4.a. through 4.i.)** of this form.

4.a. In Care of Name

4.b. Street Number and Name

4.c. Apt. ☐ Ste. ☐ Flr. ☐

4.d. City or Town

4.e. State **4.f.** Zip Code

4.g. Postal Code

4.h. Province

4.i. Country

4.j. Daytime Phone Number ( ) -

Part 8. Signature of Applicant *(Read the information on penalties in the Form instructions before completing this Part.)* If you are filing for a Re-entry Permit or Refugee Travel Document, you must be in the United States to file this application.

1.a. I certify, under penalty of perjury under the laws of the United States of America, that this application and the evidence submitted with it is all true and correct. I authorize the release of any information from my records that U.S. Citizenship and Immigration Services needs to determine eligibility for the benefit I am seeking.

Signature of Applicant

1.b. Date of Signature *(mm/dd/yyyy)* ▶

2. Daytime Phone Number ( ) -

NOTE: If you do not completely fill out this form or fail to submit required documents listed in the instructions, your application may be denied.

Part 9. Information About Person Who Prepared This Application, If Other Than the Applicant

NOTE: If you are an attorney or representative, you must submit a completed Form G-28, Notice of Entry of Appearance as Attorney or Accredited Representative, along with this application.

Preparer's Full Name

Provide the following information concerning the preparer:

1.a. Preparer's Family Name *(Last Name)*

1.b. Preparer's Given Name *(First Name)*

2. Preparer's Business or Organization Name

Preparer's Mailing Address

3.a. Street Number and Name

3.b. Apt. ☐ Ste. ☐ Flr. ☐

3.c. City or Town

3.d. State **3.e.** Zip Code

3.f. Postal Code

3.g. Province

3.h. Country

Preparer's Contact Information

4. Preparer's Daytime Phone Number ( ) - Extension

5. Preparer's E-mail Address *(if any)*

Declaration

To be completed by all preparers, including attorneys and authorized representatives: I declare that I prepared this benefit request at the request of the applicant, that it is based on all the information of which I have knowledge, and that the information is true to the best of my knowledge.

6.a. Signature of Preparer

6.b. Date of Signature *(mm/dd/yyyy)* ▶

NOTE: If you require more space to provide any additional information, use a separate sheet of paper. You must include your Name and A-Number on the top of each sheet.

Affidavit of Support Under Section 213A of the INA

Department of Homeland Security
U.S. Citizenship and Immigration Services

USCIS
Form I-864
OMB No. 1615-0075
Expires 07/31/2017

For USCIS Use Only	Affidavit of Support Submitter	Section 213A Review	Number of Support Affidavits in File
	☐ Petitioner ☐ 1st Joint Sponsor ☐ 2nd Joint Sponsor ☐ Substitute Sponsor ☐ 5% Owner	☐ MEETS requirements ☐ DOES NOT MEET requirements Reviewed By: ____________ Office: ____________ Date (mm/dd/yyyy): ________	☐ 1 ☐ 2 **Remarks**

▶**START HERE - Type or print in black ink.**

Part 1. Basis For Filing Affidavit of Support

I, ______________________________,
am the sponsor submitting this affidavit of support because (Select **only one** box):

1.a. ☐ I am the petitioner. I filed or am filing for the immigration of my relative.

1.b. ☐ I filed an alien worker petition on behalf of the intending immigrant, who is related to me as my ______________________________

1.c. ☐ I have an ownership interest of at least 5 percent in ______________________________ which filed an alien worker petition on behalf of the intending immigrant, who is related to me as my ______________________________

1.d. ☐ I am the only joint sponsor.

1.e. ☐ I am the ☐ first ☐ second of two joint sponsors.

1.f. ☐ The original petitioner is deceased. I am the substitute sponsor. I am the intending immigrant's ______________________________

NOTE: If you select Item Number 1.a., 1.b., 1.c., 1.d., 1.e., or 1.f., you must include proof of your U.S. citizenship, U.S. national status, or lawful permanent resident status.

Part 2. Information About the Principal Immigrant

1.a. Family Name (Last Name) ______________________________

1.b. Given Name (First Name) ______________________________

1.c. Middle Name ______________________________

Mailing Address

2.a. In Care Of Name ______________________________

2.b. Street Number and Name ______________________________

2.c. ☐ Apt. ☐ Ste. ☐ Flr. ____________

2.d. City or Town ______________________________

2.e. State ______ **2.f.** ZIP Code ____________

2.g. Province ______________________________

2.h. Postal Code ______________________________

2.i. Country ______________________________

Part 2. Information About the Principal Immigrant (continued)

Other Information

3. Country of Citizenship or Nationality

4. Date of Birth (mm/dd/yyyy)

5. Alien Registration Number (A-Number) (if any)
▶ A-

6. USCIS ELIS Account Number (if any)
▶

7. Daytime Telephone Number

Part 3. Information About the Immigrants You Are Sponsoring

1. I am sponsoring the principal immigrant named in **Part 2.**
☐ Yes ☐ No (Applicable only if you are sponsoring family members in **Part 3.** as the second joint sponsor)

2. ☐ I am sponsoring the following family members immigrating at the same time or within six months of the principal immigrant named in **Part 2.** (Do not include any relative listed on a separate visa petition.)

Family Member 1

3.a. Family Name (Last Name)

3.b. Given Name (First Name)

3.c. Middle Name

4. Relationship to Sponsored Immigrant

5. Date of Birth (mm/dd/yyyy)

6. Alien Registration Number (A-Number) (if any)
▶ A-

7. USCIS ELIS Account Number (if any)
▶

Family Member 2

8.a. Family Name (Last Name)

8.b. Given Name (First Name)

8.c. Middle Name

9. Relationship to Sponsored Immigrant

10. Date of Birth (mm/dd/yyyy)

11. Alien Registration Number (A-Number) (if any)
▶ A-

12. USCIS ELIS Account Number (if any)
▶

Family Member 3

13.a. Family Name (Last Name)

13.b. Given Name (First Name)

13.c. Middle Name

14. Relationship to Sponsored Immigrant

15. Date of Birth (mm/dd/yyyy)

16. Alien Registration Number (A-Number) (if any)
▶ A-

17. USCIS ELIS Account Number (if any)
▶

Family Member 4

18.a. Family Name (Last Name)

18.b. Given Name (First Name)

18.c. Middle Name

Part 3. Information About the Immigrants You Are Sponsoring (continued)

19. Relationship to Sponsored Immigrant

20. Date of Birth (mm/dd/yyyy)

21. Alien Registration Number (A-Number) (if any)
▶ A-

22. USCIS ELIS Account Number (if any)
▶

Family Member 5

23.a. Family Name (Last Name)

23.b. Given Name (First Name)

23.c. Middle Name

24. Relationship to Sponsored Immigrant

25. Date of Birth (mm/dd/yyyy)

26. Alien Registration Number (A-Number) (if any)
▶ A-

27. USCIS ELIS Account Number (if any)
▶

28. Enter the total number of immigrants you are sponsoring on this affidavit from **Item Numbers 1.a. - 27.**

Part 4. Information About You (Sponsor)

Sponsor's Full Name

1.a. Family Name (Last Name)

1.b. Given Name (First Name)

1.c. Middle Name

Sponsor's Mailing Address

2.a. In Care Of Name

2.b. Street Number and Name

2.c. ☐ Apt. ☐ Ste. ☐ Flr.

2.d. City or Town

2.e. State **2.f.** ZIP Code

2.g. Province

2.h. Postal Code

2.i. Country

3. Is your current mailing address the same as your physical address? ☐ Yes ☐ No

If you answered "No" to **Item Number 3.**, provide your physical address below.

Sponsor's Physical Address

4.a. Street Number and Name

4.b. ☐ Apt. ☐ Ste. ☐ Flr.

4.c. City or Town

4.d. State **4.e.** ZIP Code

4.f. Province

4.g. Postal Code

4.h. Country

For USCIS Use Only

Part 4. Information About You (Sponsor) (continued)

Other Information

5. Country of Domicile

6. Date of Birth (mm/dd/yyyy)

7. City or Town of Birth

8. State or Province of Birth

9. Country of Birth

10. U.S. Social Security Number (Required) ▶

Citizenship or Residency

11.a. ☐ I am a U.S. citizen.

11.b. ☐ I am a U.S. national.

11.c. ☐ I am a lawful permanent resident.

12. Sponsor's A-Number (if any) ▶ A-

13. Sponsor's USCIS ELIS Account Number (if any) ▶

Military Service (To be completed by petitioner sponsors only.)

14. I am currently on **active duty** in the U.S. Armed Forces or U.S. Coast Guard. ☐ Yes ☐ No

Part 5. Sponsor's Household Size

NOTE: Do not count any member of your household more than once.

Persons you are sponsoring in this affidavit:

1. Provide the number you entered in **Part 3., Item Number 28.**

Persons NOT sponsored in this affidavit:

2. Yourself. 1

3. If you are currently married, enter "1" for your spouse.

4. If you have dependent children, enter the number here.

5. If you have any other dependents, enter the number here.

6. If you have sponsored any other persons on Form I-864 or Form I-864 EZ who are now lawful permanent residents, enter the number here.

7. **OPTIONAL:** If you have siblings, parents, or adult children with the same principal residence who are combining their income with yours by submitting Form I-864A, enter the number here.

8. Add together **Part 5., Item Numbers 1. - 7.** and enter the number here. **Household Size:** 1

For USCIS Use Only

Part 6. Sponsor's Employment and Income

I am currently:

1.a. ☐ Employed as a/an

1.a.1. Name of Employer 1 (if applicable)

1.a.2. Name of Employer 2 (if applicable)

1.b. ☐ Self employed as a/an (Occupation)

1.c. ☐ Retired From (Company Name)

since (mm/dd/yyyy)

1.d. ☐ Unemployed

since (mm/dd/yyyy)

2. My current individual annual income is:

$

Income you are using from any other person who was counted in your household size, including, in certain conditions, the intending immigrant. (See Form I-864 Instructions.) Please indicate name, relationship, and income.

Person 1

3. Name

4. Relationship

5. **Current Income** $

Person 2

6. Name

7. Relationship

8. **Current Income** $

Person 3

9. Name

10. Relationship

11. **Current Income** $

Person 4

12. Name

13. Relationship

14. **Current Income** $

15. **My Current Annual Household Income** (Total all lines from **Part 6., Item Numbers 2., 5., 8., 11.**, and **14.**; the total will be compared to Federal Poverty Guidelines on Form I-864P.) $

16. ☐ The people listed in **Item Numbers 3., 6., 9.**, and **12.** have completed Form I-864A. I am filing along with this affidavit all necessary Form I-864As completed by these people.

For USCIS Use Only	Household Size	Poverty Guideline	Remarks
	☐ 1 ☐ 2 ☐ 3 ☐ 4 ☐ 5 ☐ 6 ☐ 7 ☐ 8 ☐ 9 ☐ Other______	Year: 20____ Poverty Line: $__________	

Part 6. Sponsor's Employment and Income (continued)

17. ☐ One or more of the people listed in **Item Numbers 3., 6., 9.**, and **12.** do not need to complete Form I-864A because he or she is the intending immigrant and has no accompanying dependents.

Name ______________________

Federal Income Tax Return Information

18.a. Have you filed a Federal income tax return for each of the three most recent tax years? ☐ Yes ☐ No

NOTE: You **MUST** attach a photocopy or transcript of your Federal income tax return for only the most recent tax year.

18.b. ☐ (Optional) I have attached photocopies or transcripts of my Federal income tax returns for my second and third most recent tax years.

My total income (adjusted gross income on Internal Revenue Service (IRS) Form 1040EZ) as reported on my Federal income tax returns for the most recent three years was:

	Tax Year	Total Income
19.a. Most Recent		$
19.b. 2nd Most Recent		$
19.c. 3rd Most Recent		$

20. ☐ I was not required to file a Federal income tax return as my income was below the IRS required level and I have attached evidence to support this.

Part 7. Use of Assets to Supplement Income (Optional)

If your income, or the total income for you and your household, from Part 6., Item Numbers 19.a. - 19.c., exceeds the Federal Poverty Guidelines for your household size, YOU ARE NOT REQUIRED to complete this Part 7. Skip to Part 8.

Your Assets (Optional)

1. Enter the balance of all savings and checking accounts. $ ________

2. Enter the net cash value of real-estate holdings. (Net value means current assessed value minus mortgage debt.) $ ________

3. Enter the net cash value of all stocks, bonds, certificates of deposit, and any other assets not already included in **Item Number 1.** or **Item Number 2.** $ ________

4. **Add together Item Numbers 1. - 3. and enter the number here.** TOTAL: $ ________

Assets from Form I-864A, Part 4., Item Number 3.d., for:

5.a. Name of Relative ______________________

5.b. Your household member's assets from Form I-864A (optional). $ ________

Assets of the principal sponsored immigrant (optional). The principal sponsored immigrant is the person listed in **Part 2., Item Numbers 1.a. - 1.c.**

6. Enter the balance of the sponsored immigrant's savings and checking accounts. $ ________

For USCIS Use Only	Household Size	Poverty Guideline	Sponsor's Household Income (Page 5, Line 10)	Remarks
	☐ 1 ☐ 2 ☐ 3 ☐ 4 ☐ 5 ☐ 6 ☐ 7 ☐ 8 ☐ 9 ☐ Other______	Year: 20__	$______	
		Poverty Line: $______	*The total value of all assets, line 10, must equal 5 times (3 times for spouses and children of USC's, or 1 time for orphans to be formally adopted in the U.S.) the difference between the poverty guidelines and the sponsor's household income, line 10.*	

Part 7. Use of Assets to Supplement Income (Optional) (continued)

7. Enter the net cash value of all the sponsored immigrant's real estate holdings. (Net value means investment value minus mortgage debt.)
$ ______

8. Enter the current cash value of the sponsored immigrant's stocks, bonds, certificates of deposit, and other assets not included in **Item Number 6.** or **Item Number 7.**
$ ______

9. **Add together Item Numbers 6. - 8. and enter the number here.**
$ ______

Total Value of Assets

10. **Add together Item Numbers 4., 5.b., and 9. and enter the number here.** **TOTAL: $** ______

Part 8. Sponsor's Contract, Statement, Contact Information, Certification, and Signature

NOTE: Read the information on penalties in the **Penalties** section of the Form I-864 Instructions before completing this part.

Sponsor's Contract

Please note that, by signing this Form I-864, you agree to assume certain specific obligations under the Immigration and Nationality Act (INA) and other Federal laws. The following paragraphs describe those obligations. Please read the following information carefully before you sign Form I-864. If you do not understand the obligations, you may wish to consult an attorney or accredited representative.

What is the Legal Effect of My Signing Form I-864?

If you sign Form I-864 on behalf of any person (called the intending immigrant) who is applying for an immigrant visa or for adjustment of status to a lawful permanent resident, and that intending immigrant submits Form I-864 to the U.S. Government with his or her application for an immigrant visa or adjustment of status, under INA section 213A, these actions create a contract between you and the U.S. Government. The intending immigrant becoming a lawful permanent resident is the consideration for the contract.

Under this contract, you agree that, in deciding whether the intending immigrant can establish that he or she is not inadmissible to the United States as a person likely to become a public charge, the U.S. Government can consider your income and assets as available for the support of the intending immigrant.

What If I Choose Not to Sign Form I-864?

The U.S. Government cannot make you sign Form 1-864 if you do not want to do so. But if you do not sign Form I-864, the intending immigrant may not become a lawful permanent resident in the United States.

What Does Signing Form I-864 Require Me to do?

If an intending immigrant becomes a lawful permanent resident in the United States based on a Form I-864 that you have signed, then, until your obligations under Form I-864 terminate, you must:

A. Provide the intending immigrant any support necessary to maintain him or her at an income that is at least 125 percent of the Federal Poverty Guidelines for his or her household size (100 percent if you are the petitioning sponsor and are on active duty in the U.S. Armed Forces or U.S. Coast Guard, and the person is your husband, wife, or unmarried child under 21 years of age); and

Part 8. Sponsor's Contract, Statement, Contact Information, Certification, and Signature (continued)

B. Notify U.S. Citizenship and Immigration Services (USCIS) of any change in your address, within 30 days of the change, by filing Form I-865.

What Other Consequences Are There?

If an intending immigrant becomes a lawful permanent resident in the United States based on a Form I-864 that you have signed, then, until your obligations under Form I-864 terminate, the U.S. Government may consider (deem) your income and assets as available to that person, in determining whether he or she is eligible for certain Federal means-tested public benefits and also for state or local means-tested public benefits, if the state or local government's rules provide for consideration (deeming) of your income and assets as available to the person.

This provision does **not** apply to public benefits specified in section 403(c) of the Welfare Reform Act such as emergency Medicaid, short-term, non-cash emergency relief; services provided under the National School Lunch and Child Nutrition Acts; immunizations and testing and treatment for communicable diseases; and means-tested programs under the Elementary and Secondary Education Act.

What If I Do Not Fulfill My Obligations?

If you do not provide sufficient support to the person who becomes a lawful permanent resident based on a Form I-864 that you signed, that person may sue you for this support.

If a Federal, state, local, or private agency provided any covered means-tested public benefit to the person who becomes a lawful permanent resident based on a Form I-864 that you signed, the agency may ask you to reimburse them for the amount of the benefits they provided. If you do not make the reimbursement, the agency may sue you for the amount that the agency believes you owe.

If you are sued, and the court enters a judgment against you, the person or agency that sued you may use any legally permitted procedures for enforcing or collecting the judgment. You may also be required to pay the costs of collection, including attorney fees.

If you do not file a properly completed Form I-865 within 30 days of any change of address, USCIS may impose a civil fine for your failing to do so.

When Will These Obligations End?

Your obligations under a Form I-864 that you signed will end if the person who becomes a lawful permanent resident based on that affidavit:

A. Becomes a U.S. citizen;

B. Has worked, or can receive credit for, 40 quarters of coverage under the Social Security Act;

C. No longer has lawful permanent resident status and has departed the United States;

D. Is subject to removal, but applies for and obtains, in removal proceedings, a new grant of adjustment of status, based on a new affidavit of support, if one is required; or

E. Dies.

NOTE: Divorce **does not** terminate your obligations under Form I-864.

Your obligations under a Form I-864 that you signed also end if you die. Therefore, if you die, your estate is not required to take responsibility for the person's support after your death. However, your estate may owe any support that you accumulated before you died.

Sponsor's Statement

NOTE: Select the box for either **Item Number 1.a.** or **1.b.** If applicable, select the box for **Item Number 2.**

1.a. ☐ I can read and understand English, and have read and understand every question and instruction on this affidavit, as well as my answer to every question.

1.b. ☐ The interpreter named in **Part 9.** has also read to me every question and instruction on this affidavit, as well as my answer to every question, in ______________________, a language in which I am fluent. I understand every question and instruction on this affidavit as translated to me by my interpreter, and have provided complete, true, and correct responses in the language indicated above.

Part 8. Sponsor's Contract, Statement, Contact Information, Certification, and Signature (continued)

2. ☐ I have requested the services of and consented to ____________________, who ☐ is ☐ is not an attorney or accredited representative, preparing this affidavit for me.

Sponsor's Contact Information

3. Sponsor's Daytime Telephone Number

4. Sponsor's Mobile Telephone Number (if any)

5. Sponsor's Email Address (if any)

Sponsor's Certification

Copies of any documents I have submitted are exact photocopies of unaltered, original documents, and I understand that USCIS or the Department of State may require that I submit original documents to USCIS or the Department of State at a later date. Furthermore, I authorize the release of any information from any and all of my records that USCIS or the Department of State may need to determine my eligibility for the benefit that I seek.

I furthermore authorize release of information contained in this affidavit, in supporting documents, and in my USCIS or Department of State records to other entities and persons where necessary for the administration and enforcement of U.S. immigration laws.

I certify, under penalty of perjury, that the information in my affidavit and any document submitted with my affidavit were provided by me and are complete, true, and correct, and:

A. I know the contents of this affidavit of support that I signed;

B. I have read and I understand each of the obligations described in **Part 8.**, and I agree, freely and without any mental reservation or purpose of evasion, to accept each of those obligations in order to make it possible for the immigrants indicated in **Part 3.** to become lawful permanent residents of the United States;

C. I agree to submit to the personal jurisdiction of any Federal or state court that has subject matter jurisdiction of a lawsuit against me to enforce my obligations under this Form I-864;

D. Each of the Federal income tax returns submitted in support of this affidavit are true copies, or are unaltered tax transcripts, of the tax returns I filed with the IRS;

E. I understand that, if I am related to the sponsored immigrant by marriage, the termination of the marriage (by divorce, dissolution, annulment, or other legal process) will not relieve me of my obligations under this Form I-864; and

F. I authorize the Social Security Administration to release information about me in its records to the Department of State and USCIS.

Sponsor's Signature

6.a. Sponsor's Signature

➡

6.b. Date of Signature (mm/dd/yyyy)

NOTE TO ALL SPONSORS: If you do not completely fill out this affidavit or fail to submit required documents listed in the Instructions, USCIS or the Department of State may deny your affidavit.

Part 9. Interpreter's Contact Information, Certification, and Signature

Provide the following information about the interpreter.

Interpreter's Full Name

1.a. Interpreter's Family Name (Last Name)

1.b. Interpreter's Given Name (First Name)

2. Interpreter's Business or Organization Name (if any)

Interpreter's Mailing Address

3.a. Street Number and Name

3.b. ☐ Apt. ☐ Ste. ☐ Flr.

3.c. City or Town

3.d. State **3.e.** ZIP Code

3.f. Province

3.g. Postal Code

3.h. Country

Interpreter's Contact Information

4. Interpreter's Daytime Telephone Number

5. Interpreter's Email Address (if any)

Interpreter's Certification

I certify that:

I am fluent in English and ______, which is the same language provided in **Part 8., Item Number 1.b.**;

I have read to this sponsor every question and instruction on this affidavit, as well as the answer to every question, in the language provided in **Part 8., Item Number 1.b.**; and

The sponsor has informed me that he or she understands every instruction and question on the affidavit, as well as the answer to every question, and the sponsor verified the accuracy of every answer.

Interpreter's Signature

6.a. Interpreter's Signature

6.b. Date of Signature (mm/dd/yyyy)

Part 10. Contact Information, Statement, Certification, and Signature of the Person Preparing this Affidavit, If Other Than the Sponsor

Provide the following information about the preparer.

Preparer's Full Name

1.a. Preparer's Family Name (Last Name)

1.b. Preparer's Given Name (First Name)

2. Preparer's Business or Organization Name (if any)

Part 10. Contact Information, Statement, Certification, and Signature of the Person Preparing this Affidavit, If Other Than the Sponsor (continued)

Preparer's Mailing Address

3.a. Street Number and Name

3.b. ☐ Apt. ☐ Ste. ☐ Flr.

3.c. City or Town

3.d. State **3.e.** ZIP Code

3.f. Province

3.g. Postal Code

3.h. Country

Preparer's Contact Information

4. Preparer's Daytime Telephone Number

5. Preparer's Fax Number

6. Preparer's Email Address (if any)

Preparer's Statement

7.a. ☐ I am not an attorney or accredited representative but have prepared this affidavit on behalf of the sponsor and with the sponsor's consent.

7.b. ☐ I am an attorney or accredited representative and my representation of the sponsor in this case ☐ extends ☐ does not extend beyond the preparation of this affidavit.

NOTE: If you are an attorney or accredited representative whose representation extends beyond preparation of this affidavit, you must submit a completed Form G-28, Notice of Entry of Appearance as Attorney or Accredited Representative, with this affidavit.

Preparer's Certification

By my signature, I certify, swear, or affirm, under penalty of perjury, that I prepared this affidavit on behalf of, at the request of, and with the express consent of the sponsor. I completed this affidavit based only on responses the sponsor provided to me. After completing the affidavit, I reviewed it and all of the responses with the sponsor, who agreed with every answer on the affidavit. If the sponsor supplied additional information concerning a question on the affidavit, I recorded it on the affidavit.

Preparer's Signature

8.a. Preparer's Signature

8.b. Date of Signature (mm/dd/yyyy)

Part 11. Additional Information

If you need extra space to provide any additional information within this affidavit, use the space below. If you need more space than what is provided, you may make copies of this page to complete and file with this affidavit or attach a separate sheet of paper. Include your name and A-Number (if any) at the top of each sheet; indicate the **Page Number, Part Number,** and **Item Number** to which your answer refers; and sign and date each sheet.

Your Full Name

1.a. Family Name (Last Name)

1.b. Given Name (First Name)

1.c. Middle Name

2. A-Number (if any) ▶ A-

3.a. Page Number **3.b.** Part Number **3.c.** Item Number

3.d.

4.a. Page Number **4.b.** Part Number **4.c.** Item Number

4.d.

5.a. Page Number **5.b.** Part Number **5.c.** Item Number

5.d.

2016 HHS Poverty Guidelines for Affidavit of Support

Department of Homeland Security
U.S. Citizenship and Immigration Services

USCIS
Form I-864P
Supplement

2016 HHS Poverty Guidelines*

Minimum Income Requirements for Use in Completing Form I-864

For the 48 Contiguous States, the District of Columbia, Puerto Rico, the U.S. Virgin Islands, Guam, and the Commonwealth of the Northern Mariana Islands:

Sponsor's Household Size	100% of HHS Poverty Guidelines*	125% of HHS Poverty Guidelines*
	For sponsors on active duty in the U.S. Armed Forces who are petitioning for their spouse or child	*For all other sponsors*
2	$16,020	$20,025
3	$20,160	$25,200
4	$24,300	$30,375
5	$28,440	$35,550
6	$32,580	$40,725
7	$36,730	$45,912
8	$40,890	$51,112
	Add $4,160 for each additional person.	Add $5,200 for each additional person.

For Alaska:

Sponsor's Household Size	100% of HHS Poverty Guidelines*	125% of HHS Poverty Guidelines*
	For sponsors on active duty in the U.S. Armed Forces who are petitioning for their spouse or child	*For all other sponsors*
2	$20,020	$25,025
3	$25,200	$31,500
4	$30,380	$37,975
5	$35,560	$44,450
6	$40,740	$50,925
7	$45,920	$57,400
8	$51,120	$63,900
	Add $5,200 for each additional person.	Add $6,500 for each additional person.

For Hawaii:

Sponsor's Household Size	100% of HHS Poverty Guidelines*	125% of HHS Poverty Guidelines*
	For sponsors on active duty in the U.S. Armed Forces who are petitioning for their spouse or child	*For all other sponsors*
2	$18,430	$23,037
3	$23,190	$28,987
4	$27,950	$34,937
5	$32,710	$40,887
6	$37,470	$46,837
7	$42,230	$52,787
8	$47,010	$58,762
	Add $4,780 for each additional person.	Add $5,975 for each additional person.

Means - Tested Public Benefits

Federal Means-Tested Public Benefits. To date, Federal agencies administering benefit programs have determined that Federal means-tested public benefits include Food Stamps, Medicaid, Supplemental Security Income (SSI), Temporary Assistance for Needy Families (TANF), and the State Child Health Insurance Program (SCHIP).

State Means-Tested Public Benefits. Each State will determine which, if any, of its public benefits are means-tested. If a State determines that it has programs which meet this definition, it is encouraged to provide notice to the public on which programs are included. Check with the State public assistance office to determine which, if any, State assistance programs have been determined to be State means-tested public benefits.

Programs Not Included: The following Federal and State programs are **not** included as means-tested benefits: emergency Medicaid; short-term, non-cash emergency relief; services provided under the National School Lunch and Child Nutrition Acts; immunizations and testing and treatment for communicable diseases; student assistance under the Higher Education Act and the Public Health Service Act; certain forms of foster-care or adoption assistance under the Social Security Act; Head Start Programs; means-tested programs under the Elementary and Secondary Education Act; and Job Training Partnership Act programs.

*** These poverty guidelines remain in effect for use with Form I-864, Affidavit of Support, from March 1, 2016 until new guidelines go into effect in 2017.**

Sample Notice of Action

Department of Homeland Security
U.S. Citizenship and Immigration Services

I-797, Notice of Action

THE UNITED STATES OF AMERICA

RECEIPT NUMBER WAC-16-902- 08501		CASE TYPE I130 PETITION FOR ALIEN RELATIVE
RECEIPT DATE December 15, 2015	PRIORITY DATE December 14, 2015	PETITIONER
NOTICE DATE January 12, 2016	PAGE 1 of 1	BENEFICIARY
TONISHA GILLIARD		**Notice Type:** Approval Notice Section: Husband or wife of U.S. Citizen, 201(b) INA

This notice is to advise you of action taken on this case. The official notice has been mailed according to the mailing preferences noted on the Form G-28, Notice of Entry of Appearance as Attorney or Accredited Representative. Any relevant documentation was mailed according to the specified mailing preferences.

The above petition has been approved. We have sent the original visa petition to the **Department of State National Visa Center (NVC), 32 Rochester Avenue, Portsmouth, NH 03801-2909**. NVC processes all approved immigrant visa petitions that need consular action. It also determines which consular post is the appropriate consulate to complete visa processing. NVC will then forward the approved petition to that consulate.

The NVC will contact the person for whom you are petitioning(beneficiary) concerning further immigrant visa processing steps.

You should allow a minimum of 30 days for Department of State processing before contacting the NVC. If you have not received any correspondence from the NVC within 30 days, you may contact the NVC by e-mail at NVCINQUIRY@state.gov. You will need to enter the USCIS receipt number from this approval notice in the subject line. In order to receive information about your petition, you will need to include the Petitioner's name and date of birth, and the Applicant's name and date of birth, in the body of the e-mail.

The approval of this visa petition does not in itself grant any immigration status and does not guarantee that the alien beneficiary will subsequently be found to be eligible for a visa, for admission to the United States, or for an extension, change, or adjustment of status.

This courtesy copy may not be used in lieu of official notification to demonstrate the filing or processing action taken on this case.

THIS FORM IS NOT A VISA AND MAY NOT BE USED IN PLACE OF A VISA.

NOTICE: Although this application/petition has been approved, USCIS and the U.S. Department of Homeland Security reserve the right to verify the information submitted in this application, petition and/or supporting documentation to ensure conformity with applicable laws, rules, regulations, and other authorities. Methods used for verifying information may include, but are not limited to, the review of public information and records, contact by correspondence, the internet, or telephone, and site inspections of businesses and residences. Information obtained during the course of verification will be used to determine whether revocation, rescission, and/or removal proceedings are appropriate. Applicants, petitioners, and representatives of record will be provided an opportunity to address derogatory information before any formal proceeding is initiated.

EIP
EASY IMMIGRATION
PUBLICATIONS

SAMPLE

Please see the additional information on the back. You will be notified separately about any other cases you filed.
USCIS
CALIFORNIA SERVICE CENTER
P. O. BOX 30111
LAGUNA NIGUEL CA 92607-0111
Customer Service Telephone: (800) 375-5283

Form I-797 (Rev. 01/31/05) N

Sample Green Card

Front

Rear